MW00856992

WORLD DIRECTORS SERIES

Film retains its capacity to beguile, entertain and open up windows onto other cultures like no other medium. Nurtured by the growth of film festivals worldwide and by cinephiles from all continents, a new generation of directors has emerged in this environment over the last few decades.

This new series aims to present and discuss the work of the leading directors from across the world on whom little has been written and whose exciting work merits discussion in an increasingly globalised film culture. Many of these directors have proved to be ambassadors for their national film cultures as well as critics of the societies they represent, dramatising in their work the dilemmas of art that are both national and international, of local relevance and universal appeal.

Written by leading film critics and scholars, each book contains an analysis of the director's works, filmography, bibliography and illustrations. The series will feature film-makers from all continents (including North America), assessing their impact on the art form and their contribution to film culture.

Other Titles in the Series

Shyam Benegal
Jane Campion
Youssef Chahine
Yash Chopra
Atom Egoyan
Emir Kusturica
Lars von Trier

Forthcoming:
Pedro Almodóvar
Mike Leigh
Terrence Malick
Kitano Takeshi

WONG KAR-WAI

Stephen Teo

 Publishing

For Bea

First published in 2005 by the
BRITISH FILM INSTITUTE
21 Stephen Street, London W1T 1LN

The British Film Institute promotes greater understanding
of, and access to, film and moving image culture in the UK.

Illustrations: BFI Stills; Media Asia: pp. 18, 19, 21, 26, 27, 28, 35, 40, 42

Cover design by Ketchup
Cover image: *2046* (Wong Kar-wai, 2004), Block 2 Pictures/Paradis Films/Orly Films/Jet Tone
Set by couch
Printed in the UK by The Cromwell Press, Trowbridge, Wiltshire

British Library Cataloguing-in-Publication Data
A catalogue record for this book is available from the British Library

ISBN 1–84457–029–0 (pbk)
ISBN 1–84457–028–2 (hbk)

CONTENTS

AUTHOR'S NOTE AND ACKNOWLEDGMENTS

In writing this book, I have relied on many Chinese-language source materials, all quotes from which (including dialogue from Wong's films) are my own translations. The titles of all Chinese sources in the Notes and Bibliography are rendered in Pinyin according to the Mandarin pronunciations. All the Chinese names of Hong Kong personalities in the book are transliterated according to their Cantonese tones, while names otherwise pronounced in Mandarin are transliterated in Pinyin, with the exception of the names of Taiwanese personalities (e.g. Chang Chen, whose name in Pinyin is 'Zhang Zhen').

I wish to extend my sincere gratitude to all those who have facilitated the writing of this book: Sophia Contento, Andrew Lockett, Philippa Hawker, Patrick Tam, Michael Campi, Bono Lee, Sam Ho and Delphine Ip. Above all, I wish to thank Winnie Fu for acting as my liaison in Hong Kong, and my wife Bea-fung for her invaluable support.

One
Introduction

Star of the Hong Kong–Global Nexus

Wong Kar-wai is one of a handful of Hong Kong Chinese directors whose name is readily recognised in the West. Without having to adopt a Western first name (like 'John' Woo, or 'Bruce' Lee), Wong Kar-wai has come to signify a cool, post-modern sensibility in world cinema. However, as a Chinese name that is moreover rendered in Cantonese phonetics (in Mandarin, Wong's name is pronounced 'Wang Jiawei'), 'Wong Kar-wai' sounds exotic, foreshadowing a highly local sensibility rather than a global phenomenon. It may be a truism to state that the cinema of Wong Kar-wai is a conglomeration of Eastern and Western features, but the name of Wong Kar-wai, taken in itself, is like a riddle wrapped in an enigma. How do we understand Wong Kar-wai as a Hong Kong film-maker? How do we reconcile Wong's global standing with his local roots? Can Wong's art be said to be both local and global at the same time? It will be the purpose of this book to resolve the riddle and the enigma of Wong Kar-wai.

We might begin with the proposition that Wong is a transcendent film-maker on two counts: first, though his films have brought wider attention to the Hong Kong cinema, he is able to rise above his Hong Kong identity and excel beyond the pulp-fiction limitations of genre that seem to tie down much of Hong Kong cinema; second, as a post-modern artist in Western eyes, his films exceed facile stereotypes of the delicate and exotic East. Wong Kar-wai's name may sound exotic, but the fact that Wong has won critical recognition throughout the world infers a state of mutual acceptance and absorption of East and West. However, this may in fact mirror the state of Hong Kong's own condition as a city straddling East and West, for Wong's films are firmly grounded in Hong Kong. In the cinema of Wong Kar-wai, Hong Kong and the cinema are conjoined as one. It is a dynamic interactive force; but while Wong's films assume the kind of restless energy of the city itself, they also display obvious signs of what we may call systemic flaws, such as lack of discipline, a chronic inability to work according to predetermined scripts and derivative influences. Strengths and weaknesses are interrelated and they seem more formally ingrained in Wong's works, although they are certainly not unique to the director. They remain a part of Wong's creative make-up because they stem from the environment of the film industry in which he works.

Wong therefore embodies a contradiction or paradox. He is a Hong Kong film-maker who cannot disentangle himself from the system but who is widely recognised around the world for his unconventional style of cinema. Wong's films come out of the capitalist-industrial complex supporting the mainstream Hong Kong cinema, but his films resist the mainstream. Hong Kong itself has proved resistant to his films, as judged on the whole by their consistently poor domestic box-office earnings. His most approving audience is found generally outside Hong Kong. Wong's market is therefore the world, which appreciates him as an arthouse director; and Wong has survived as a film-maker because of this. This paradox illustrates the director's complexity as a film-maker and the challenge that it poses in analysing his career.

This book will trace the genesis of Wong's cinema by acknowledging his local roots and by examining his influences, which are not merely cinematic but also literary. Wong's lineage lies not only in the Hong Kong cinema but also in foreign and local literature. It is this mixture of cinematic and literary influences that makes him a distinctive Hong Kong post-modern stylist. To begin first with the cinematic influences, David Bordwell and Ackbar Abbas, two of Wong's more perceptive critics, have shown how he is indebted to the Hong Kong genre cinema. Bordwell states that Wong 'came out of mass entertainment' and that his films are 'firmly rooted in genres'.[1] Abbas makes the same point more or less when analysing the director's first four films: 'Each starts with the conventions of a popular genre – and deliberately loses its way in the genre'.[2] Both critics see Wong as a child of the Hong Kong genre cinema and correctly analyse how the director feeds off this industry and is nurtured by it.

Indeed, it is worth our while to run through just what kinds of genres Wong's films belong to. *As Tears Goes By* is a gangster movie in the mould of Scorsese and John Woo; it is also a romance melodrama. *Days of Being Wild* is an 'Ah Fei' movie-cum-romance ('Ah Fei' being a distinctive Cantonese genre, and slang for young ruffian or discontented punk). *Chungking Express* is a light romance with touches of noir intrigue (at least in the first part of the movie featuring Brigitte Lin, whose iconic presence evokes more the romantic melodramas of the 1970s with which she made her name). *Ashes of Time* is a *wuxia* (martial chivalry) movie with characters culled from a popular martial arts novel. *Fallen Angels* starts off as a movie about a professional killer and changes direction into various strands of melodrama (including a father-and-son relationship movie). *Happy Together* is a gay road movie romance trailing a pre-1997 anomie theme. *In the Mood for Love* is a *wenyi* film in the classic style, indicating a melodrama with Chinese characteristics, fundamentally a love story about repressed desire.

From these descriptions, while it is true that all these films are essentially genre films that fall within the traditions of Hong Kong cinema, it is equally true that they are transformed by Wong's iconoclastic approach, such that it is possible to insist that they are not genre films, although they may be implicit tributes to the forms and conventions of genre film-making in the Hong Kong cinema. Bordwell and Abbas praise Wong's singular style as a film-maker, which they see as rooted in genre or mutations of genres, but they neglect Wong's literary influences and their role in determining the style and structures of his films. The premise that Wong's films are rooted in literature is one that remains basically undeveloped in critical analysis of the director, a deficiency that I will attempt to rectify here.[3] In considering Wong as a director with a literary bent, I hasten to add that his films are not literary adaptations in the Merchant–Ivory mould or that his is the kind of cinema that equates film with literature. Rather, Wong's model is someone like Alain Resnais, a film-maker who appropriates literary subjects from authors such as Jean Cayrol, Alain Robbe-Grillet, Marguerite Duras, David Mercer and Alan Ayckbourn, and transforms their writings and themes into images of pure cinema through composition, lighting and camera movements. Wong's literariness is a sensibility of telling stories in cinematic style.

Wong Kar-wai in auteur mood

Wong's literariness is also marked by highly literate and poetic dialogue, which is influenced by his avid reading of Latin American authors such as Manuel Puig and Julio Cortázar, the Japanese author Haruki Murakami and local Hong Kong authors like Jin Yong and Liu Yichang. How these authors shape Wong's films will be fully discussed in the following chapters as I analyse each of his films closely. Though Wong's interest in literature is wide – he has also cited authors like Raymond Chandler, Gabriel García Márquez and Osamu Dazai – the one author who seems to have influenced him most deeply is Manuel Puig. It was Patrick Tam, an iconoclastic director in his own right with whom Wong worked and who acted as his mentor in the early stage of his career, who had introduced Wong to Puig's *Heartbreak Tango*, since when, according to Tam, Wong has tried to 'master the structure' of the novel by applying it to his movies.[4]

Wong may well be the Manuel Puig of Hong Kong cinema. Because he is usually regarded as a visual stylist and Hong Kong cinema itself is characterised by physical action that has little time for psychological portrayal, it is often forgotten how literary Wong can be. The comparison with Puig alludes to the seminal nature of the author's influence and the way that Wong has digested his style of storytelling. However, given that Puig shows a clear indebtedness to cinema in his novels (inscribed as they are by excessive references to film narratives and stars), the literary nature of the author's influence on Wong is deceptive but not out of place. Wong has tried to master not only Puig's structures (induced by fragmented and impressionistic memories of films) but the whole concept of monologues as narrative devices reinforcing and pushing the episodic nature of his cinema into psychological and poetic realms. While the interior nature of Wong's work, illustrated by his monologues, conveys an intimate quality, his visual skills often involve a large and complex palette incorporated in a canvas and design of epic proportions. The encompassing of both an intimate literary quality and a structurally complex epic design in his work illustrates a 'discontinuity in our very being', to use the words of Michel Foucault. I invoke Foucault's perspective of 'effective history' as the critical approach of this book. 'Effective history' is opposed to 'traditional history', which aims at 'dissolving the singular event into an ideal continuity – as a teleological movement or a natural process'.[5]

In examining Wong's career as 'effective history', the implication is that he has had a far from smooth relationship with the Hong Kong film industry. The relationship is ruptured and discontinuous, to the extent that he is both a quintessential Hong Kong director and a maverick who bucks the system. It also relates to the way that Wong looks at the history of Hong Kong and its cinema, and how this history plays out through time and memory, which is his most effective theme. Like the narrator in Proust's *Remembrance of Things Past*, Wong strives to achieve a transmutation of memory into being, setting his memory in motion in the medium of the cinema.

Wong is nostalgically associated with a past filtered through the prism of the Hong Kong cinema. All of his films show in varying degrees a cinephiliac strain that harks back to a certain memory of a cinema that, although in the past, still retains its appeal in the mind of the film-maker. In films like *Days of Being Wild* and *In the Mood for Love*, he also re-creates the Hong Kong of his childhood. This suggests that Wong cannot be sepa-

rated from his Hong Kong heritage, which places him firmly in the generation of Hong Kong film-makers who share a concern for Hong Kong as a
geographical and historical entity – a view that Abbas has propounded
through a theory of a 'space of the *déjà disparu*'.[6] The theory indicates a heritage always in danger of disappearing due to Hong Kong's special position
as a post-modern city perched between East and West, where its space
becomes 'difficult to represent in terms of traditional realism', because
history goes through 'strange loops'.[7] Abbas includes Wong among a generation of Hong Kong film-makers whose films have tried to retrieve the
culture or heritage of the *déjà disparu*. Wong responds to an urge to retrieve
this culture in an unpredictable fashion but with an acute sensitivity that
belies his pop-art style.

Wong's style in all its fragmented post-modern fervour, lends itself to a
facile reading of his films. His detractors accuse him of being shallow, but
this study will have no truck with that notion. Far from being shallow,
Wong's films form a considerable body of work that flows from the cultural
roots embedded deep within the Hong Kong cinema, as well as from his own
psyche. Insofar as this is a critical study and not merely a retrospective look
at Wong's films, it is a history that falls within the perspective of an alternative cinema culture that signals a certain opposition to European high art
and Hollywood low art. Our current understanding of this alternative film
culture is still plainly inadequate.

The perception of Wong's shallowness may explain why there has been
no book-length study of his films up to now. Wong himself tends to reinforce the impression of the shallow film-maker by playing up his image as a
media celebrity. Entertainment and gossip columns generally emphasise
the glitzy appeal of the director (who wears eye-catching dark glasses in
public). The articles gloss up his employment of big stars and the length of
time that he expends on shooting his films (a source of consternation for his
stars, often leading to reports of disputes between actors and director).
However, Wong is something of a celebrity in the world of academia as well.
His films are included in university film courses everywhere. Students find
him a popular and appealing subject for essays and theses. Though serious
analytical pieces on Wong have been published in magazines, academic

journals and anthologies, no writer has yet attempted a sustained textual analysis of his entire oeuvre. Again, this may reflect how Wong is viewed in bits and pieces, much like his films; or it may be a delayed reaction to another charge that tends to follow him, which is that he is an overrated talent.

Given that this is effectively the first full-length book study of Wong Kar-wai, the premise here is that we are only beginning to rate him in a serious and meticulous fashion. Wong merits a critical study of this kind not only because he is a major talent in current world cinema but also because it is a rare talent in the context of the Hong Kong film industry. He is the only contemporary director who seems able to buck the system, beating the industry at its own game without, so far, suffering the consequences (of being unemployed, for example, because of his reputation for waste and tardiness). Most Hong Kong directors work fast and cheaply, whereas Wong spends tens of millions of dollars on each of his most recent projects and takes his time. He is probably the only director who can spend two years on a project, as he did on *In the Mood for Love*, and impose his own deadline. When I wrote this, Wong was still working on *2046*, a project begun some four years ago and then put aside in order to shoot *In the Mood for Love*. This is already a record of sorts. The only precedent for this in Hong Kong occurred during the shooting of King Hu's martial arts masterpiece *A Touch of Zen* (1968–72). Hu was criticised for his fastidious methods, and, up to a point, was ostracised by the major studios, after which his career never fully recovered.

Wong has his share of ungenerous critics inside the industry, but he has kept on working virtually as an independent since *Days of Being Wild*, which was a huge financial write-off for its production company In-Gear. Wong might not have recovered from the fiasco if not for the fact that he was and is a good player of politics in the industry, and that he had a powerful friend and backer behind him at the time, namely Jeff Lau, a director of commercial hits and his partner in In-Gear, who virtually guaranteed his career from then on. Lau had apparently guaranteed *Days of Being Wild* by persuading Alan Tang, the major partner who bankrolled the project, that he would cover its losses by making another film for the company that would be a sure-fire hit. Wong's friendship with Jeff Lau has endured to this day, and their association symbolises the kind of symbiosis that the Hong Kong film industry has come to rely upon, where one director is known for purely commercial films, the other for iconoclastic 'art' films. Such a symbiosis shows how Wong was able to rely on the commercial industry as a means to realise his dreams, while giving something back to the industry by supervising overtly commercial projects such as the 2002 Chinese New Year holiday movie *Chinese Odyssey 2002*, directed by Lau, to offset his image as an uncommercial director.

The shape of the industry has changed from King Hu's time, when an artist of Hu's calibre could not be accommodated by the system, to one where an artist of Wong's ability can call the shots and play the game adroitly within the industry. The reality is that since Wong came into critical prominence in the early 1990s, the film industry has been plagued by a shrinking regional market that resulted from the financial meltdown in the economies of the area. It is easy to dismiss Wong's long shooting schedules and his impromptu working style as irresponsible in the light of this economic crisis, but he is a director who goes against the grain of slipshoddiness, seven-day wonders (or the practice of shooting a film quickly, as fast as a week in the old days) and a system dominated by producers and compromised by powerful big-name stars. Aesthetically, Wong set the standards of painstaking craftsmanship in *mise en scène*, production design, cinematography, editing and music. He also sets another standard by blending literature and cinema through the evocative use of voiceover monologues, giving each character an interior voice and a point of view that makes them stakeholders in the narrative – singling him out as a rare literary stylist as well as a visual one.

Wong has so far completed eight feature films that are quite extraordinary for their capacity to excite the senses and the intellect, and for the ease with which they cross over from local to global nuances. His meticulous working method may seem to belie the facility of his narratives, as they give the impression of being concocted seemingly out of the creative blue: *Chungking Express* is a prime example of this. Indeed, Wong made the film in fewer than three months while taking a break from the arduous and prolonged schedule of *Ashes of Time*, proof that he can work fast if necessary.

On the other hand, a film like *2046* now serves as the model of Wong's tardiness in completing a film due to his habit of working extempore and his quest for perfectionism. Wong worked on the film in fits and starts over five years, wandering around the region shooting and re-shooting scattered scenes, changing the plot, and juggling the conflicting schedules of his stars, some of whom were rumoured to have walked out, unhappy about his methods. The SARS outbreak in 2003 caused further delays, and in the midst of this, Wong found time to shoot and complete a short film *The Hand*, his contribution in a three-part omnibus film. *2046* was completed in 2004, almost on the eve of its release in China and Hong Kong over the Mid-Autumn Festival holiday period in September. Wong had kept working on the film even after its exposure at the Cannes Film Festival, which accommodated the director's tardiness by changing its own schedule.

It is perhaps best to see Wong's slow and protracted production schedules through the looking-glass of a style of film-making that has a time-honoured line: one could cite Erich von Stroheim and the making of *Greed* (1925), Orson Welles's *Othello* (1952) and *Don Quixote* (1957), and King Hu's *A Touch of Zen* (1969), as well as the fastidious methods of Terrence Malick, Martin Scorsese, Michael Powell and David Lean. One could also point to the experimental avant-garde cinema: for example, Harry Smith's *Mahagonny* (1980), a massive visual translation of Weill and Brecht's opera *The Rise and Fall of the City of Mahagonny*, which was constructed from eleven hours of footage shot over a period of ten years. On the intimate scale, Wong's style may be likened to the Dogme school without the dogma; the minimalism of Suzuki, Antonioni, Godard, Bresson, Ruiz and Jarmusch; and the free improvisatory style of independent film-makers like John Cassavetes and Rob Nilsson.

Wong's talent is evidently marked by an eclecticism and heterogeneity that combines not only East and West, the local and the global, the literary and the cinematic, but several streams of film traditions and styles by reaching back into the repertoire of old conventions and genres. All of this ultimately makes Wong a typical Hong Kong director who has fitted into the production system despite accusations that his fastidious methods and per-

ceived esoteric or avant-garde quality are incompatible with that system.
Wong has shown that he cannot do without the industry, and that the industry cannot do without him – at least up to the present.

The Advent of Wong Kar-wai

Wong Kar-wai was born in 1958 in Shanghai. He moved to Hong Kong when
he was five years old. According to an interview with Wong published in the
New York-based *Bomb Magazine*, his father was an ex-sailor, who later
worked as a nightclub manager, and his mother a housewife.[8] From what can
be discerned in *Days of Being Wild* and *In the Mood for Love*, both films that
could be described as roughly autobiographical, scenes of nightclubs, gos-
siping housewives playing mahjong and living the life of a sailor drifting
from one place to another, are the kinds of experiences of growing up that
are etched in Wong's creative subconscious. In addition, Shanghai is also an
important and distinctive presence in these films, representing a community that spoke an utterly different dialect from the Cantonese.

The Shanghainese who poured into the territory before and after the
Communists took over China in 1949 brought with them not only their cap-
ital and skills in all kinds of industry but also a way of life. As Wong has said:
'They had their own cinema, their own music, and their own rituals.'[9] The
Shanghainese cinema is actually a reference to the Mandarin film industry
in Hong Kong, which, in the 1950s, tended to produce ersatz Shanghai films
as if the industry was still centred in Shanghai pre-1949, with stories set in
its environs, and characters who exhibited a lifestyle and fashions that
underlined their homesickness for the city. Typical of this style are the
films of Zhou Xuan, a Shanghainese singer and actress who made several
films in the territory between 1947 and 1949, and who is invoked as an
iconic presence in *In the Mood for Love* through the use of old standards
(Zhou's song 'Huayang de Nianhua', which she sang in a 1947 movie, is
actually the Chinese title of Wong's film and is heard briefly on the radio in
a scene) and the wearing of the *cheongsam*, the tight-fitting dress worn in
gorgeous harmony on the person of Maggie Cheung and a fashion associated with the women of Shanghai. Here, Wong's memory of his mother
(who died before he made his first film) has probably played an informa-

tive role, as borne out by his remark that he didn't have to do any research for Cheung's *cheongsam* wardrobe, 'because our mothers dressed like this'.[10]

While the Shanghainese attempted to build a Shanghai in Hong Kong, Hong Kong eventually exerted its own reality and assimilated the Shanghainese. By the 1960s, the Mandarin cinema had made a transition from a conscious nostalgia for Shanghai to a fuller integration with Hong Kong and its environment. The Mandarin film industry had by this time been taken over by two overseas Chinese moguls – Loke Wan Tho and Run Run Shaw – who did not feel as attached to Shanghai because they came from Southeast Asia (though Shaw had Shanghai connections, he had been based in Singapore and Malaysia for some time). The characters in Mandarin films increasingly acknowledged Hong Kong not as a place of exile but a destination to put down roots.

Wong has spoken of feeling isolated as a Shanghainese child living in Cantonese-speaking Hong Kong, and it may be said that this perception has translated into his status as a maverick film-maker in the Hong Kong film industry. On the other hand, like most mainland migrants who grew up in Hong Kong, Wong has assimilated into Hong Kong Cantonese society, and his films also reflect this condition. Part of the pleasure of watching a film like *Days of Being Wild* is aural – hearing the spoken Cantonese of 1960s' Hong Kong characters incarnated by Leslie Cheung, Maggie Cheung, Jacky Cheung and Andy Lau, all of whom speak in natural conversational tones caught in synchronous sound recording (a practice that only became the norm in the Hong Kong film industry in the 1990s; prior to that, the industry had mostly employed post-synch dubbing). The Cantonese milieu is as natural to Wong as his Shanghai background, but other elements that contributed to his formative character in this period can also be glimpsed from the aural construct of *Days of Being Wild* – namely, the Latin music, the Philippines connection. Hong Kong was and remains a compendium of many communities and cultures. The Latin beat that sounds pervasively in *Days of Being Wild*, *Happy Together* and *In the Mood for Love* – all three films forming a 'Latin trilogy'– is an offshoot of the Hong Kong Filipino band culture as well as the popularity of Latin

American pop music filtered through Hollywood and the global reach of American music corporations.

Southeast Asia is a lingering presence in Wong's films (besides the Philippines in *Days of Being Wild*, there is Singapore and Cambodia in *In the Mood for Love*), which I believe is his way of representing the multicultural reality of Hong Kong. Southeast Asia also represents a search for cultural identity, partly manifested by the theme of drifting. In *Days of Being Wild*, unable to fulfil his love for Maggie Cheung, Andy Lau gives up his job as a cop to become a sailor and ends up in the Philippines; in *In the Mood for Love*, Tony Leung plays a roving journalist, a sailor of sorts, drifting from place to place after experiencing a similar unfulfilled love for Maggie Cheung; and in *Happy Together*, Leslie Cheung and Tony Leung are a pair of modern wanderers in Argentina. All of this may be associated with the fact that Wong's father was a sailor, which he alludes to in a number of interviews without going into too much detail.[11] *Fallen Angels* contains a revealing depiction of a father-and-son relationship as an easygoing and sentimental mutual attachment, which probably has parallels with Wong's real-life relationship with his father. According to Wong, his father (who died after Wong made his second film) wrote two scripts that he might shoot one day: one of the scripts is based on his father's experiences as a sailor.[12]

The painstaking methods Wong employed in creating the Hong Kong of the 1960s in *Days of Being Wild*, *In the Mood for Love* and *2046* betray a certain regression to his childhood in more than an impressionistic form. In fact, they denote a certain obsession with the past and an indication that the 1960s continue to resonate in his psyche. The latter film was an accurate portrayal of Wong's cramped living quarters, with 'neighbours living next door ... on the other side of the wall ... And there was a lot of gossip and it was fun.'[13] In this context, the Hong Kong of the 1960s, which has practically vanished today, is the 'disappeared space' alluded to by Abbas as a strategy of representing the *déjà disparu*, with its attendant political connotations of mutations in society and values lost.

In the Mood for Love stops in 1966 in its current version, but it was originally meant to end in 1972. Wong shot some scenes that took place in 1972, but finally deleted them from the film.[14] From this we might conclude that the 1970s appear not to resonate in the same way as the 1960s in Wong's consciousness, and he has not referred specifically to the decade in any profound way in his interviews or films. It was probably an uneventful period when he would have gone through primary and secondary schooling, but nevertheless, it is a gap that could justify the writing of a proper biography of Wong in the future.

Wong graduated in 1980 from the Hong Kong Polytechnic, where he studied graphic design. His professional life began the following year when he joined TVB, Hong Kong's premier TV station. Having received training in writing and directing, he was put to work, under the tutelage of Kam Kwok-leong, as a writer and production assistant on two TV series. By 1982, he had joined the film industry as a scriptwriter. Wong contributed ideas in a collective way to a script rather than as an autonomous writer. He worked in all kinds of genres, including romance, comedy, horror crossed with comedy, cop thrillers, gangster pictures and fantasy adventure – the sort of 'mass entertainment' that Bordwell identifies as Wong's lineage.

Wong's working style as a director is a product of this lineage – the fact that he generally liked to combine genres and to start shooting films without a completed script. Patrick Tam states that Wong never finished a script when he was a scriptwriter, and that the nearest he came was the screenplay of *Final Victory* (1987). But even here, Tam asserts, the script was actually finished by Tam himself in collaboration with Winnie Yu, his associate producer, when Wong failed to keep to the deadline.[15] Tam achieved a rapport with Wong as a writer, but seldom had intellectual discussions with him about Tam's own films: 'Wong was more of an instinctive creative person given to emotional bonding.' *Final Victory* was the first collaboration between the two men. Tam would go on to edit *Days of Being Wild* and *Ashes of Time*. While it is tempting to trace how the creative partnership between the two men might have been seeded in their work on *Final Victory* (which will be discussed in more detail in the next chapter), Tam discourages any parallels between Wong's work and his own. Rather, it would seem that their association was more a case of an older professional acting as a mentor to a younger, upcoming professional, offering him a guiding hand within the industry, and introducing him to the literature of Manuel Puig and

Raymond Chandler (whose influence informs the noir sensibility of Wong's BMW short film *The Follow* [2001]).

Wong's other partnership in this early stage of his career was with Jeff Lau. Their paths crossed in the mid-1980s when they were both moving in and out of various production companies (Century, D and B, Wing Scope, In-Gear) and writing scripts on a regular basis with the aim of becoming directors. Lau made the transition to directing in 1987, apparently with Wong's mentorship, and he became known for his farcical comedies such as *All for the Winner* (1990) and *The Top Bet* (1991), which were huge box-office hits. While Wong appears to be Lau's polar opposite, he has continued the relationship by writing a few scripts for Lau, the most striking of which was the action fantasy *Saviour of the Soul* (1991). But even though their films are radically different, they share a complementary rhythm and a peculiar obsession with time and space. Lau has even produced his own responses to Wong's films by making versions of *Days of Being Wild* (Lau's version being *Days of Tomorrow* [1993]) and *Ashes of Time* (his versions being *The Eagle Shooting Heroes* [1994] and *A Chinese Odyssey, Parts One and Two* [1996]). A sense of mutual indebtedness is inherent in the relationship, and Lau facilitated Wong's debut as a director by convincing Alan Tang, a former actor turned producer, to invite Wong Kar-wai to become a partner in the newly formed In-Gear film company. It was for In-Gear that Wong made *As Tears Go By* in 1988, the film that launched his directing career.

Two
In Mainstream Gear: *As Tears Go By* (1988)

Gangster in Love and War

For the seekers of the *Dao* of Wong Kar-wai's cinema, *As Tears Go By* would at first seem to be a work of minor significance, suggesting none of the mystery to come, and offering only minimal signs of the director's style. There is none of the narrative fragmentation, none of the temporal and spatial constructions, or the monologic ruminations of Wong's second film *Days of Being Wild* and the subsequent films. *As Tears Go By* is like a stripling compared with these other works. Yet, the devoted among the seekers may not wish to pass it by and they could do no worse than see the film as a preparatory step in the quest for the final epiphany in Wong's cinema, for the film suggests an awareness of the nature of the Hong Kong cinema that Wong actively sought to counteract in his subsequent works.

The nature of Hong Kong cinema concerns the way the industry follows commercial trends and makes films according to a formula, which involved, as Wong put it, 'telling a story with appropriate this and appropriate that'.[1] The trend in the late 1980s, which Wong was as obliged to follow as other directors, was the production of numerous triad gangster movies focusing on the theme of brotherhood based on the concept of chivalric justice and righteousness, known in Chinese as *yi*. Clearly, *As Tears Go By* is a conventional film, but one that Wong had to make in order to prove himself to the industry. He was, after all, a junior partner in In-Gear, the company that produced it. Before letting him direct *As Tears Go By*, the company had assigned Wong to *Flaming Brothers* (1987), a gangster movie with a touch of romance based on the generic brotherhood formula, which he had scripted and also produced.[2] Prior to that, his only experience in the genre was his screenplay of Patrick Tam's *Final Victory*, which can be seen as a dry run for

As Tears Go By. In fact, Wong has gone on record as saying that the two films are 'close to each other'.[3]

Both films are set in the same gangland milieu – sleazy, neon-lit Mongkok in deepest Kowloon – and both films also deal with the theme of a tutelary relationship between a gangster 'big brother' and a junior sibling. *Final Victory* opens with 'big brother' Bo (played by the director Tsui Hark) delivering an object lesson in macho behaviour to junior brother Hung (Eric Tsang). Bo then entrusts two of his girlfriends to the care of Hung while he serves out a jail sentence. One of the girls, Ping (Margaret Lee), owes money to a rival boss, while the other, Mimi (Li Lai-zhen), ends up in a peep-show parlour in Tokyo. It is up to Hung to save both women from humiliation in order to maintain his big brother's reputation, but the women scorn Hung all the more for his inability to stand up to Bo. Hung must also keep the women in the dark about the fact that each is Bo's mistress. Eventually, Hung falls in love with Mimi, posing the dilemma that he has now betrayed the trust of his big brother. Mimi reciprocates Hung's love and reveals their affair to Bo, who vows to kill Hung when he gets out.

Patrick Tam sees no similarity between *Final Victory* and *As Tears Go By*; rather he believes that the central relationship in the latter film was inspired by the Harvey Keitel–Robert De Niro pairing in Martin Scorsese's *Mean Streets* (1973).[4] Wong, however, maintains that both his scripts were part of a trilogy that he had developed from a news item about adolescent youths who had been groomed by triads to become assassins and who carried out their mission after a night of fun and revelry.[5] Set in the Mongkok underworld, the characters progressed from youth to adulthood. *As Tears Go By* was the first episode, substantiated by Wong's claim that he already had an outline of the script before he wrote *Final Victory*.[6] Hence, the relationship between the 'big brother' gangster Wah (Andy Lau) and his junior brother Fly (Jacky Cheung) in *As Tears Go By* was in fact meant as the prototype of the Tsui Hark–Eric Tsang relationship in *Final Victory*.

Tam also points out that Wong had more than one American model in mind.[7] The premise of the plotline between Wah and his cousin Ngor (Maggie Cheung), who has come from Lantau Island to stay briefly in Wah's apartment in the city, was based on Jim Jarmusch's *Stranger Than Paradise*

(1984), which features a female protagonist who travels from Hungary to visit her cousin in New York; she then leaves for Cleveland, setting in motion a road movie in which the cousin and a buddy drive to wintry Cleveland to look for her; once together, they decide to go to sunny Florida.

The fusion of characters from *Mean Streets* and *Stranger Than Paradise*, two quite different films, sets up a certain tension between the two pairs of relationships. There are compatible crosscurrents between Hong Kong and American gangster pictures, but the Jarmusch film seems somehow anomalous, fitting uneasily into the mix. Wong somehow manages to make it work for his film. He achieved this essentially by adjusting his mix of genres, drawing on the traditions of the Chinese cinema even when he is appropriating American genres. Wong adjusted Jarmusch's road movie by transforming it into a Taiwanese-type sentimental romance, featuring teenagers or young adults (often starring Brigitte Lin) and containing inserted song numbers done in the pre-MTV style, a genre that Wong claimed was more suited to his temperament when treated realistically.[8] The permutations in the interchange of the gangster and the romance genres form the experimental basis of *As Tears Go By* and are what make the film interesting.

The gangster plot wholly revolves around the duet of Wah and Fly, and the latter's attempts to make good in Wah's eyes, but whose erratic behaviour hinders his progress. Wah is constantly forced either to stop Fly from overreacting or to save the situation when he does. Eventually, Fly is put to work as an illegal street hawker selling fishballs, but he finds the experience humiliating. Fly borrows money from Tony (Alex Man), a rival 'big brother' and protector of a mahjong joint, but when he is unable to pay the exorbitant interest, Wah, as Fly's tutelary 'big brother', is drawn into the conflict. This leads to a stand-off between Wah and Tony. A series of battles of one-upmanship follows, climaxing in the brutal beating Wah and Fly receive at the hands of Tony and his gang in an alley.

To redeem himself as well as Wah's reputation in the gangster community, Fly resolves to take on a job to assassinate a fellow gangster turned police witness. He confronts Tony one last time, exposing the latter's cowardice and meanness in front of his men. Vindicated, Fly prepares to carry

Big brother and junior: Andy Lau and Jacky Cheung in *As Tears Go By*

out the assassination but is cornered by Wah, who tries to talk him out of it. The dialogue is rich with heartfelt moments as both men practically plead with each other, but the edge is with Fly:

> FLY: Let me do it just this once! I'd rather be a hero for a day than a fly for a lifetime.
>
> WAH: All right, if you must do it, I'll go with you. I'll be your back-up, so that if you are shot, I'll finish the job.
>
> FLY: Don't be so good to me, I beg of you! I can't pay you back!

This heated exchange (in which, Jacky Cheung gives what is perhaps his most riveting performance) acutely captures the essence of the gangster mythology as manifested in the Hong Kong cinema. Fly's aspiration to be a hero is a reference passed down from the trend of 'hero movies' sparked off by John Woo's *A Better Tomorrow* (1986) (the Chinese title of which translates as 'The Essence of Heroes'), which contains similar heart-stopping stretches of dialogue between sworn and blood brothers concerning honour, duty, loyalty and death (or the willingness to die) as the final vindica-

Jacky Cheung's apotheosis: *As Tears Go By*

tion of heroism. According to this generic formula, Wong's film appropri-
ately ends with the assassination scene, where Fly only wounds his target
and is himself shot and killed by the police; Wah completes the job, but he
too is killed.[9]

Wong has acquitted himself well in grasping the genre's hero mythology
and handling its elements of action and violence. But the central relationship between Wah and Fly remains an enigma. Why should Wah be so pro-
tective of Fly, who is clearly bent on self-destruction? The emotional core of
this relationship is not fully explained, nor is it framed within a moral argument, as in Scorsese's depiction of the relationship between Charlie (Keitel)
and Johnny Boy (De Niro) in *Mean Streets*. According to Patrick Tam:

> I remember telling Wong Kar-wai after seeing the film that *Mean Streets* had a
> point: its moral sense was derived from Christianity. Harvey Keitel seeks to
> redeem himself through his protection of De Niro as a sacrifice, an answer to
> God, and this is signalled in the beginning with Keitel going to confession. This
> moral framework is lost when transposed to the Hong Kong context.[10]

Tam is right in suggesting that the basic male relationship in *As Tears Go By* simply lacks the depth of that in *Mean Streets*, but an audience familiar with the brotherhood mythology of the Hong Kong gangster movie and its reliance on the concept of yi, which obliges brothers to act within a moral-ethical code, may just accept that Wah acts with the same sense of moral guilt that Charlie displays. However, it is just as valid to say that Wong derived from *Mean Streets* not so much the basic outline of the relationship between Charlie and Johnny Boy but the essence of Scorsese's treatment of this relationship, basing a narrative on characters and developing it according to the vagaries of emotional relationships. Wong had his own rationale for the emotional relationships in the film:

> It's very difficult to describe why a man likes a woman, and the deep feelings between two brothers, and so on. They are all very subtle. But I wanted to put forward the proposition that *time is the biggest factor. The relationship between people is like opening a calendar.* You leave your trace on each day. Emotions come without your being aware of them. I don't know why I want to help you, but I've done it. (my emphasis)"

Wong's explanation of time as a factor in relationships and emotions is better demonstrated in the romantic component of the film, which apparently begins as a romance. Wah, who sleeps by day and wakes at night, receives a phone call from his aunt informing him that his cousin Ngor must stay at his place for a few days so that she can visit the doctor for a check-up. This whole first sequence, obviously based on the first section of *Stranger Than Paradise* (even down to the detail of giving the aunt an accent: in Jarmusch's film, the aunt has a Hungarian accent, here she speaks with a Hakka accent), centres on the motif of phone conversations, which deftly introduce Wah's relationships with first Ngor and then Fly. All three characters are therefore established, although Fly is heard but not seen.

No sooner has Wah put the phone down than Ngor turns up at the door, wearing a face mask. She is the very picture of a weak, consumptive girl redolent of the kind of suffering female familiar from countless romance melodramas featuring lovers, one of whom is terminally ill; except here, Ngor's illness is not terminal (she is eventually given a clean bill of health).

Ngor's frail appearance betokens an existentialist romance that breaks the routine of Wah's life.

The romance plot is really the lynchpin of the picture, and it determines the diachronic structure of the narrative. The gangster scenes quite literally intrude into the romance: Wah is continually pulled away from Ngor by Fly, first by his constant phone calls in the opening scenes, then by his unpredictable behaviour and his demands on Wah's time. In a sense, the film, which starts out as a romance (as denoted in the first instance by its borrowed English title 'As Tears Go By'),[12] is thrown off balance by the gangster sequences. Wah, however, is the pivot of the film, since his separate relationships with Fly and Ngor unify the gangster and the romantic strands of the plot. At the same time, he symbolises the friction between the two strands. Wah's relationship with Ngor is hardly complemented by his relationship with Fly, and in the final analysis, his relationship with Fly is more important to him, since it bears on questions of life and death. However, Ngor's presence in Wah's life has clearly left a mark on him. Thus, when she returns to Lantau Island, where she works in a restaurant, Wah has already become smitten with her.

Passionate embrace: Andy Lau and Maggie Cheung in *As Tears Go By*

Wah decides to chase after Ngor by making the trip to Lantau, where he discovers that she is being courted by a young doctor. Disheartened, he waits to depart on the ferry. But Ngor then leaves a message on his pager (a marker of the times before mobile phones became the norm) asking him to wait at the pier. She returns; there is a brief moment of suspense as the pier seems to be deserted; then suddenly, Wah grabs her hand from behind and runs towards a phone booth, where they kiss passionately, to the strains of the Canto-pop version of 'Take My Breath Away' that overlays the whole sequence. Their affair comes rather late in the picture, and the dialogue illustrates this awareness of the time dimension: 'Why did you leave it so late?' Ngor asks Wah. 'Because I know myself,' Wah replies, 'and I don't want to make any promises. If I didn't miss you, I won't look for you.'

Time Delayed

Knowledge of oneself, promises and feelings are associated with time, or rather lateness, which is time delayed, time wasted. Already in *As Tears Go By*, we see the first indication of Wong's preoccupation with time – and it is worthwhile to point out that Maggie Cheung appears to be the character-bearer of this motif, extending it from *As Tears Go By* to *Days of Being Wild* and *In the Mood for Love*. Cheung's first appearance in the film, distinguished by her sickly and fragile demeanour, suggests that time is not on her side. Any relationship with her would be a brittle one, a theme countenanced in the first scenes between Ngor and Wah, when Wah's attitude towards her is distinctly nonchalant. The change in their relationship is gradual and slow, typified by brusque communication and even a moment of hostility when Wah returns home in a drunken rage one night, smashing glasses and over-turning tables, following a confrontation with his girlfriend in which she had taunted him with the disclosure that she had aborted his child. 'Have you lost your lover?' Ngor asks innocently, which sets off a violent response from Wah. 'Never say that!' Wah retorts, as he pins Ngor to the wall.

Such a violent response is not out of character for Wah, but it is meant effectively as a touch of irony signalling the romance that will actually develop between the two. This is further underscored by the symbolism of Ngor's departing gift to Wah of a set of glasses, following the verdict that she is in good health: she hides one glass for him to find, because she knows that he will break all the others. He does find the glass, and brings it with him on his journey to Lantau. The brittleness of their relationship is symbolised by this glass, which he throws into the water following his discovery that she is being courted by the doctor.

The final irony in this romance is that it is Wah whose life will be cut short. His terminal condition, however, stems not from poor health – he is in fact incredibly fit and shows a knack for surviving and recovering from the worst of beatings and torture – but from the social environment of his gangster life. Ngor is aware that Wah's profession makes him vulnerable and, in fact, she feels the first pangs of love for him after the incident in which Wah kills the snooker king who has humiliated Fly by publicly beating him up on the streets of Mongkok. Much later, Ngor nurses Wah back to health after his own beating at the hands of Tony and his gang. Wah's vulnerability underscores the time element in his relationship with Ngor, who seems resigned to losing him – a pattern of behaviour that is not so curious with hindsight, as we can now link Ngor with the other characters Maggie Cheung plays in the series of films that she made for Wong Kar-wai.

Still, in *As Tears Go By*, her aura of resignation betrays the note of doomed romance that provides the key to the whole film. Here, the lovers are somehow aware of their fates, or, at least, one partner is aware that the other will die. Ngor's question, 'Why did you leave it so late?', assumes a certain epigraphic significance. The awareness that theirs is a love that has come so late, and that time is of the essence, explains Ngor's readiness to consummate her affair with Wah. Not that Ngor does not harbour doubts about Wah: witness the scene where Ngor hesitates slightly on the stairs before ascending to Wah's room, recalling the episode in *In the Mood for Love* in which Maggie Cheung's character trots up and down the hotel stairs, trying to decide whether or not she should go into Tony Leung's room, its jagged intensity matched by Wong's use of jump-cuts.

Ngor does not turn back and descend the stairs. Wong has shaped his characters as people who 'do things that they shouldn't be doing'.[13] Wong explains:

Maggie Cheung shouldn't be with Andy Lau. He is a temptation to her, and she ends up not getting him. Fly attempts to do things beyond his capabilities, but he never stops trying. Andy Lau shouldn't be protecting Jacky Cheung, but he can't do otherwise.[14]

Hence, *As Tears Go By* is a film modulated by its characters, as Wong has maintained: 'My film doesn't have a story, the plot is entirely developed from the characters. I feel that the story isn't important, the characters are important.'[15] Wong also commented that he wanted to project 'his own emotions into the inner threads of the characters'.[16] Thus, we get the impression that his characters exist in their own right because of their emotions, and that they exist seemingly independent of the plot or the story. There is an essentially phenomenological thrust to Wong's films, because his characters are simply there, on the screen.

While *As Tears Go By* may be a project that emerged from the same treadmill of mainstream fare that its production company In-Gear was devoted to making, it finally stands on its own as a stylish, well-made piece supporting both the brotherhood mythology of gangster films and the tragic love-story conventions of romance films. What makes it distinctive is Wong's devotion to characters. However, the most striking achievement of the film is his visual style. We can detect the first brush strokes of pop art and MTV in Wong's cinema, the distinguishing trademarks of mass-media kitsch that are found in his later work – heralded in *As Tears Go By* in the very first opening shot showing a panoply of TV monitors making up a single screen as the credits appear.

The MTV and pop-art elements that the director injects into his narrative streams generally highlight his aesthetic credentials, but they do more than make his films look pretty (although his detractors have seized on them as indicators of his shallowness[17]). Wong's visual style is an attempt to translate innermost feelings into images: witness the action scene in which Wah kills the snooker king, which Wong renders impressionistically with the technique of stop-printing (or 'step-printing'), a process that prints selected frames in a sequence (in the colloquial expression of Hong Kong film-makers, it 'pulls' frames away from a sequence) to produce a discontinuous, strobing slow-motion effect. The same technique is used in the sequence between Wah and Ngor on the ferry pier as they run into the phone booth. In both sequences, the aesthetic of the strobing motion conveys a dreamlike and romantic sensation that we identify with the heroic protago-nist. Wah is the subjective bearer and translator of Wong's innermost feel-ings, and the strobing slow motion shows the process of the translation, as if Wong, when relieved of his feelings, draws them out in a blurred form, manifesting a discordance between impression and expression.

This discordant note invites us to look at genre conventions with slightly different eyes. Wong's visual style counteracts the seamy realism in the gangster picture and the lush sentimentality of the romance picture. For instance, colour is reduced to the minimum: red, blue and sepia. Recalling hand-tinted photography before colour photography was developed, this technique of using washed-out colours in an age when much more realistic colours are a technical possibility lends a feel of the avant-garde to the film (a technique that Wong also uses in his other films, such as *In the Mood for Love*, where, paradoxically, it evokes both nostalgia and the avant-garde).

The atmosphere of the film veers from either suppressed emotion, of things waiting to happen, to explosions of rage. The use of a limited palette, sometimes only one or two primary colours, gives interest to shots where something is about to happen (blue in the Mongkok stand-off scenes between Wah and Tony) or where the characters are waiting for each other (in the Lantau scenes between Wah and Ngor). The flat, washed-out fluo-rescent blue of the interior shots in the mahjong parlours and downmarket eateries of Mongkok are also realistic of Hong Kong and reflective of the internal emptiness of the characters' lives. In the final separation scene between Wah and Ngor on Lantau Island, a red bus functions as a percepti-ble symbol of inner emotion.

However, the manipulation of colours to reflect internal emotions does not appear to be a technique that Wong Kar-wai particularly favours: in the red bus scene, it could be argued that it is the accompanying Canto-pop song, entitled 'The Price of Infatuation', sung by Andy Lau (an obvious invocation of the MTV format following the 'Take My Breath Away' number) that plies the viewer with the sensation of emotion rather than the use of the

A classic Wong Kar-wai visual trademark: step-printed slow motion in *As Tears Go By*

The pain of separation: *As Tears Go By*

colour red itself. It is almost as if Wong is trying to lessen the distracting effects of colour without reducing the film to the monochromatic.

Wong's cameraman here was Andrew Lau, and although Wong would go on to establish a working partnership with Christopher Doyle, his collaboration with Lau in this context is significant. The cinematographic effects and the sense of colour in Lau's photography reveal the power and presence of Wong's vision that would characterise all his other films. Wong's other key collaborator is William Chang, the production designer who also edited the non-action sequences, because, according to Wong, he had the clearest understanding of the film.[18] This implicit understanding is imparted in Chang's cameo appearance in the film as the doctor who courts Ngor, and who grasps instinctively and magnanimously her feelings for Wah when she sees him at the pier, and therefore retreats into the background. Not a word is exchanged between the doctor and Ngor.

The scene works as an allegory of the kind of rapport and the level of trust that exists between Wong and Chang themselves. Their rapport, resulting in the freedom of creative input that Wong allows Chang in their films together, may have been influenced by the fact that like Wong, Chang was born in Shanghai and raised in Hong Kong, and that both started working in the film industry at about the same time.[19] More than anyone else who would collaborate with Wong on a regular basis, Chang has become the mainstay of his films, seemingly the pillar of his all-round aesthetic vision (Chang not only designs but also edits Wong's films).

There is an ascetic edge to the production design in *As Tears Go By*, a symptom perhaps of the first-time collaboration between Chang and Wong. This is demonstrated by Wah's Mongkok apartment (Wong actually shot these scenes in an apartment located in Ho Man Tin Street, near Mongkok), which looks spare and empty, with few furnishings, showing Wah's lack of commitment to a settled existence and the fact that he is a night creature who leaves his house when the sun goes down and returns to it in the day-time, but only to sleep. Such an apartment will appear again in Wong's films (*Days of Being Wild*, *Chungking Express*, *Fallen Angels*, *Happy Together* and *In the Mood for Love*), in modified forms and various states of habitation: some more cluttered, more homely, but still transient and fundamentally sad. It is a line of evolution that gains more resonance when we return to the source, to Wah's original home and its associated artefacts of betokened emptiness: the static TV screen, the broken glasses, the bare walls, and, finally, the absence of Wah himself.

As Tears Go By, therefore, wields a certain enchanting power as the harbinger of Wong's themes and characters, as well as offering a foretaste of the director's style. Even if we regard the film as a minor work, its dazzling boldness demonstrated Wong's technical capabilities and gave him the confidence to move on to his next project. In fact, there are few directors working within the mainstream Hong Kong cinema who have been able to progress so dramatically, as Wong advanced to his next, breakthrough film, *Days of Being Wild*, extending the 'inner threads' of his three main characters into the figures of Leslie Cheung, Jacky Cheung, Maggie Cheung, Andy Lau and Carina Lau, all of whom exhibit the same traits of inwardness, handsomeness and heartbreak solitariness that Wong would bring out with startling honesty and maturity.

Three

Wong's Heartbreak Tango: *Days of Being Wild* (1990)

A Rebel Puts on Wings

Days of Being Wild continues the hybrid of the gangster and romance genres from *As Tears Go By*, and it could be regarded as a work that fits into Wong's trilogy about how young people grow into gangsterism, their relationship difficulties and other tribulations, which was the original concept behind *As Tears Go By* (Chapter 2). *Days of Being Wild* was conceived as a diptych. A second part would pick up the story of the character played by Tony Leung who appears at the end of the film.[1] The plan of making a two-part film and its association with generic ideas from his first film demonstrates that Wong was clearly enamoured with the practice of serialisation right from the very start of his career – a practice that stretches back to the days of silent cinema, and indeed, is rooted in literature, reflecting Wong's adherence to the true and tried methods of storytelling.

The second part of *Days of Being Wild* was of course never made. What we have instead are characters who have devolved from *As Tears Go By*: Wah, Ngor and Fly are the precedents for Yuddy (Leslie Cheung), So Lai-chen (Maggie Cheung), and Yuddy's buddy (Jacky Cheung). Wah, Ngor and Fly go back into time, and, as it turned out, are never connected with the present.[2] The threads of a triptych have not connected and we end up with autonomous shreds, which, however, lie not in tatters but in fully spun yarns.

The narrative of *Days of Being Wild* was clearly meant to extend well beyond its frame, but the time-continuum of the ending, seemingly suspended to signal another story that has not materialised, now conveys a sense of time's eternal formlessness and the Nietzschean expectation of the 'eternal return' that Gilles Deleuze theorises about in *Difference and*

Repetition.[3] The yarn in *Days of Being Wild* transcends time, seemingly well finished but not ended. In contrast, *As Tears Go By* ends decisively, with the deaths of two key characters – an unequivocal ending, associated with the demands of the 'hero-movie' (*yingxiong pian*) genre where the death of heroes is a time-honoured principle.

The 'gangster' component of the genre admixture in *Days of Being Wild* is somewhat different from the 'hero-movie' element in *As Tears Go By*. The story is set in the 1960s, a period when the 'hero-movie' as we know it today, with its modern-day, gun-toting gangsters and choreographic violence, was not then in vogue. Rather, the gangster variation of the period was the 'Ah Fei' movie, particularly popular in the Cantonese cinema, which made its appearance following the crop of Hollywood teenage delinquent flicks influenced by the success of James Dean in Nicholas Ray's *Rebel Without a Cause* (1955).

The Ah Fei movies of the 1950s featured characters sporting James Dean hairstyles and mannerisms, but not all of them were meant to be heroes, as represented by the character actor Mak Kay. The term 'Ah Fei' denotes a young hoodlum, a delinquent or scapegrace in Cantonese, and Mak Kay personified this antisocial nature of the Ah Fei. 'Fei' literally means 'fly', a metaphor for youth old enough to sprout wings and fly away from controlling parents, and once flown, usually degenerates into socially unacceptable modes of behaviour. The term is time-specific, being generally in use in the 1950s and 60s.

The most memorable Ah Fei movies in the Cantonese cinema, such as Lung Kong's *Teddy Girls* (1969), Chor Yuen's *Joys and Sorrows of Youth* (1969), and Chan Wan's *Social Characters* (1969) (which featured Alan Tang, the executive producer of *Days of Being Wild*, in a lead role), all appeared in 1969 when Cantonese cinema was in decline and the genre, like the cinema, was going out of fashion. These films, featuring ensembles of young stars strutting their stuff, all trace the cause of young people's alienation to the failures of parents or society to respond adequately to their psychological and spiritual needs. Hence, they upheld the view that cohesive families were the bedrock of society, and that the law and the establishment were pre-eminent. Youth would have to conform or be permanently marginalised even if their antics may provide a source of entertainment for cinema audiences. Social didacticism was a characteristic of the Cantonese cinema, which finally made it unfashionable and unpalatable to the young. When the Cantonese cinema disappeared in the early 1970s, the Ah Fei genre and terminology disappeared with it. In the 1980s and 90s, it resurfaced in the form of the *gu-wak zai* (young triads) genre, reincarnated by *As Tears Go By*.

Days of Being Wild rather self-consciously alludes to the Ah Fei genre: first, in its Chinese title *A Fei Zhengzhuan* ('The Story of an Ah Fei'), which was incidentally the Chinese title for *Rebel Without a Cause* when it was released in Hong Kong. Second, Yuddy alludes to Ah Fei metaphorically in a monologue early in the film: 'I heard tell that in this world, there's a bird without legs. It can only fly and fly. When it's tired it sleeps in the wind. It lands on earth only once in its life. That is when it dies.' The bird and flight metaphor is already implicit in the Ah Fei label, which Yuddy obviously wears with some pride, and 'The Story of an Ah Fei' is his story. The fable of the bird, somewhat reminiscent of those found in the short stories of Borges, becomes a fitting epitaph for Yuddy himself.[4] The Ah Fei sobriquet, on the other hand, is a symbol of its time, like the cha-cha that Yuddy dances (to the tune of 'Maria Elena') right after uttering the monologue.

It is the time period, and the social factors with which it is associated, rather than the genre itself that is Wong's prime motivation for his own Ah Fei story. Though the film hardly seems to reference any movie of that period, it does evoke the youthful angst of rebels without causes, and in this sense it pays more of a homage to *Rebel Without a Cause* than to any of the Ah Fei movies in Hong Kong cinema. It does not require a great leap of the imagination to see that Leslie Cheung's Yuddy resembles James Dean, Jacky Cheung reminds one of Sal Mineo, while Maggie Cheung and Carina Lau merge in the Natalie Wood character. Wong pitched the movie to his stars solely on the reverberations of the Chinese title, without even a story outline. 'When I mentioned "A Fei Zhengzhuan", each person had his or her own scene in mind,' Wong said.[5] 'And just the mention of James Dean immediately sends you back to the 50s and 60s.'[6] In the final analysis, *Days of Being Wild* is less an Ah Fei movie and more an effective tribute to the whole aura and time in which the Ah Fei was active and left his or her mark on Hong Kong.

To Wong, who arrived in the territory in 1963, Hong Kong in the 1960s was particularly 'memorable, when even the sunlight seemed more abundant'.[7] The inspiration for the film was his 'special feeling' for the period.[8] Wong took great pains, spending two years and an enormous budget (HK$20 million – enormous at the time) in re-creating the decade. Given such extraordinary resources, it is perhaps little wonder that the movie has an uncanny ability to transport us back immediately to 1960 and its social confines. Indeed, 1960 stands out like a period of pure time in the film: in one instance, a cleaning woman tenderly wipes a clock hanging in the hallway outside Yuddy's apartment, almost as if she was stroking it, treasuring the time and the minutes ticking away.

Wong's memory of the 1960s is like an intaglio on his mind. To his detractors, it would seem that he simply transferred this imprint onto celluloid, lavishing time and money in the process.[9] However, the film is far more than an impression of time or memory. Wong translates time as longing. This is a story, insofar as it can be seen as a single story, of a longing for love. There is Yuddy's Oedipal longing for his mother, So Lai-chen's love for Yuddy, Lulu's (Carina Lau) love for Yuddy, Jacky Cheung's love for Lulu (or Mimi, as she lets herself be known to Cheung), the cop's (Andy Lau) love for So Lai-chen – all of which are unrequited.

Unrequited love becomes an obsession when it happens in lives that are devoid of all other ambition. Wong portrays love as a sickness, 'the destructive effects of which can be maintained for a long time', as he himself describes it.[10] Youth floating through life without an anchor is the theme of this film. But then, even the ageing Aunt (Rebecca Pan), Yuddy's surrogate mother, is searching for love. Longing in itself begets the kind of existence that the film depicts as dreamlike languor, a tropical sensation of heat and sweat that wears down all its characters. This tropical torpor quite literally saturates the whole film, conveyed in the shot of the Philippines forest of coconut and oil palm trees that appears with the title of the film, bathed in an aquamarine tint, swaying in the wind and accompanied by the mesmerising Hawaiian guitar strains of 'Always in My Heart', a number made famous by the Brazilian Indian duo, Los Indios Tabajaras.

Sensual lethargy in *Days of Being Wild*

The film, therefore, is effectively the first of Wong's mood pieces where character prevails over story. The mood casts the characters adrift in a sea of melancholia and spiritual ennui. The film takes place mostly at night. The landscape is one of vacant stairways, doorways and alleyways, where street-lights cast sharp shadows. So Lai-chen and the cop who befriends her wander, Antonioni-like, through this lonely landscape, their faces reflecting the lights of traffic passing by; an empty telephone kiosk shining like a beacon in the night assumes poignant significance (Lau waits for Lai-chen's call by this kiosk). Time is spent waiting for lovers who never come. Yuddy's rudderless existence shows itself by his favoured body postures: either reclining in chairs or on the bed. Even in the love scenes with So Lai-chen and Lulu, he is not shown actively making love, but always post-coitus, lying prone on the bed. But there is a violence that lurks behind this placid exterior: witness the scene where he attacks the gigolo for stealing Auntie's earrings. Yet these bursts of action lead nowhere and achieve little (for example, he gives the retrieved earrings to a dancing girl he wants to bed). In contrast to Andy Lau's cop-turned-sailor who tells Yuddy that he wants to 'wander about', meaning to see the world, Yuddy wants only to wander aimlessly.

In this ability to evoke the spiritual wasteland, Wong's counterpart is T. S. Eliot in poetry and Giorgio De Chirico in art, both masters at illustrating melancholia and emptiness. De Chirico's surrealist paintings had evocative and mysterious titles like *The Melancholy of Departure*, *The Nostalgia of the Infinite* and *The Uncertainty of the Poet*. De Chirico painted dreamlike pictures of silent city squares, populated by architectural structures and marble statues but no people. Similarly in *Days of Being Wild*, except for the Queen's Café scene, where some people are seen in the background, the focus in the Hong Kong segments at any one time is wholly on one or two people, at most three. It is almost as if Hong Kong is a deserted city. So Lai-chen works in a canteen at the South China Athletic Association (SCAA) football stadium (located in the Tai Hang district, Hong Kong Island), but, with the exception of Yuddy, we never see any customers, the only visible evidence of their existence being the empty Coke bottles they leave behind. With this method, Wong reinforces the social isolation of his characters. So Lai-chen is De Chirico's Ariadne [11] – her lover has deserted her too.

The film portrays human life as one of limited possibilities. We can imagine So Lai-chen spending the rest of her days collecting Coke bottles and stamping admission tickets, and sympathetically wish better things for her. It is as if by giving up on her lover and the imagined possibilities of a richer inner life that he might provide, she has surrendered to her life of shrunken horizons and sunk back into its depths. Similarly imprisoned in a life of small possibilities is Lulu. In the scene where she confronts Lai-chen in the canteen, she grips the wire fence in anguish, and it is clear to the viewer that the two girls are in some sort of mental prison, as stifling and confining as the real one.

In this film, the characters are from the struggling class: the canteen assistants, the good-time girls, cops on the beat, sailors and thieves. Trapped in their personal and social circumstances, they have difficulty mustering their energy in a positive direction, a situation made all the more poignant by the passing of time. The connection with surrealism resurfaces in the prominence given to clocks and watches. Wong's metal clocks are as persistent a presence and as symbolic as Dali's motif of soft watches in his painting *The Persistence of Memory*, indicating the malleability of time. 'Life is not long,' says Yuddy to Andy Lau on the train to nowhere in the Philippines. Even a minute can last a lifetime. The ticking of clocks is sometimes the only soundtrack we hear, evoking the melancholy of everyday existence.

Wong fixes on three o'clock in the afternoon, halfway to six o'clock and T. S. Eliot's 'burnt-out ends of smoky days';[12] halfway before night descends and the sickness of love becomes acute. Three o'clock marks the beginning of the film, the camera tracking behind Yuddy as he walks down the dark corridor into the foyer of the stadium canteen to make his play with So Lai-chen. The minute before three o'clock on 16 April, 1960, Yuddy and Lai-chen have made a compact to be friends for one minute. 'Because of you, I'll always remember this one minute,' Yuddy tells Lai-chen, and thus she is seduced. 'I've always remembered him', Lai-chen says in her monologue. In Yuddy's bed, after they have made love, she asks Yuddy, 'How long have we known each other?' 'A long time. I can't remember,' Yuddy replies. At the end of his Philippines adventure, when the Andy Lau character quizzes him discreetly as to whether he remembers what he did at three o'clock on 16 April, 1960, Yuddy reveals that he has not forgotten. 'I'll always remember what needs to be remembered. … But if you see her again, tell her I've forgotten. It's better for everybody,' he tells the sailor.

The scenes in the Philippines reinforce the idea of time spent in limbo as the experience of personal desolation and spiritual desiccation – an idea associated with tropical stupor and squalor, and represented by shots of seedy hotels and canteens, grimy arcades and stairways, prostitutes and drunk men. The sense of the tropics is equally signalled in the Hong Kong segments: Yuddy in his singlet sprawled lethargically on the bed in front of the revolving fan, the downpour of rain, the slap-slap of plastic slippers on concrete floors. In the Philippines scenes, Wong Kar-wai exhibits his fascination with locations that have been touched by Spanish influence, an outgrowth of his love of the novels of Manuel Puig and all things Latin

American. In *Days of Being Wild*, the Latin American strain is seen, and heard, in the languid sounds of the mood-guitar of Los Indios (renditions of 'Always in My Heart' and 'You Belong to My Heart') and standards by Xavier Cugat ('El Cumbanchero', 'My Shawl', 'Perfidia', 'Siboney' and 'Jungle Drums'), which add to the desultory atmosphere overlying Hong Kong and the Philippines. Puig's novels have obviously struck a chord in Wong, and it is worthwhile to recall that it was Patrick Tam who first gave Wong a copy of Puig's *Heartbreak Tango* to read. According to Tam, Wong was immediately struck by it and has since tried to 'master the structure' of the novel.[13] *Days of Being Wild* can be considered as a very loose adaptation of *Heartbreak Tango*, a novel that uncoils over time, and is told through the perspectives of a dozen or so characters in the form of letters, clippings, diary entries, police reports, even a photo album, monologues and dialogues. Wong would go on to set *Happy Together* in Argentina, his own very loose version of Puig's *The Buenos Aires Affair*.

Days of Heartbreak

Puig's novel *Heartbreak Tango* revolves around the character of Juan Carlos Etchepare, a man so devilishly handsome that he easily conquers the hearts of several women in his home town of Vallejos, including a blonde, Nené, and a brunette, Mabel. Juan Carlos, however, is a consumptive. The novel begins with his death aged twenty-nine (on the 18 April 1947) and Nené's confession, through letters of condolence to Juan Carlos's mother, that though she is now married to another man, she has never fallen out of love with Juan Carlos, who had courted her when they were both eligible for marriage. The story proceeds with time lapses, commencing and recommencing episodically, to describe the details of Juan Carlos's relationships, conducted in between rest cures at a sanatorium, with Nené (who works as a packer in the Argentine bargain store), Mabel (a teacher), Elsa (a widow), his mother and his possessive sister Celina, as well as his friendship with the Indian Pancho, a bricklayer who becomes a cop and later seduces Mabel (after having got her maid pregnant).

In the fashion of the subconscious streams of thought in which the novel is written, *Days of Being Wild* is connected with *Heartbreak Tango* in a tenta-

tive, subliminal manner. Juan Carlos Etchepare is the model for Leslie
Cheung's Yuddy. Traces of Nené and Mabel can be found in So Lai-chen and
Lulu respectively. Pancho, the bricklayer turned cop, although a more flamboyant character in Puig's novel, is manifested in *Days of Being Wild* as Andy
Lau's cop-turned-sailor, and in the Jacky Cheung character, both more
subdued figures than the ladykiller that Pancho is portrayed as in the novel.
Finally, Juan Carlos's mother and his sister Celina are combined in the
character of Rebecca Pan's surrogate mother, whose utterances reveal a personality split between maternal concern and bitchy possessiveness ('I can't
bear to give you up, because it's not worth it'). In addition, this character's
relationship with a young gigolo manifests a touch of the relationship
between the widow Elsa and Juan Carlos. The film also captures – though the
details differ – some of the everyday descriptions of life in Vallejos: the
night-time walks through the streets, the sidewalk, the trolley cars, the bars
and the bedrooms. But it is in Leslie Cheung's characterisation that the film
ultimately connects with the novel. In one of her letters, Nené writes about
how her children keep pestering her with questions:

> 'Mommy, what do you like best in the whole world?' and I immediately thought
> of one thing, but of course I couldn't say it: Juan Carlos's face. Because in my
> whole life I've never seen anything as lovely as Juan Carlos's face, may he rest in
> peace.[14]

Wong not only renders Leslie Cheung's face in close-ups or medium
close-ups in a host of scenes, but on one or two occasions, Leslie/Yuddy also
contemplates his own handsome face in mirrors as he combs his brilliantined hair, recalling Puig's description of a young man in his first novel
Betrayed by Rita Hayworth, who 'spends an hour in front of the mirror combing every single one of his little curls, longer hair than anybody in Vallejos'.[15]
Leslie/Yuddy may have straighter and shorter hair but his narcissism is all
of a piece with Puig's description.

Days of Being Wild is a veritable Leslie Cheung vanity show, in fact one of
the actor's most memorable films, in which he gives full vent to exhibiting
his beautiful face. Yuddy's awareness of his own beauty is emphasised in the
bedroom scene on the first night after he has made love to Lulu. 'Are we

going to meet again?' she asks, then gives him her telephone number. When Yuddy affects nonchalance, Lulu goes into a mock tantrum and threatens to throw acid in his face. 'Never say that!' Yuddy responds, almost hitting her. Yuddy's beautiful face is the magnet that draws women to him. Nené says of Juan Carlos, 'Women fall in love with him because he's good-looking.'[16] However, like Juan Carlos, Yuddy is in love with himself. Narcissus is deadly with women but is himself deadly ill – narcissism as a sick ego. 'He spends his life chasing women. What I can't figure out is how come they're not afraid of catching it,' Mabel retorts, referring to Juan Carlos's tuberculosis.[17] While Wong does not portray Yuddy as physically impaired, his depiction, in the Hong Kong scenes, of Yuddy's habit of endlessly lying on the bed makes him appear almost like a consumptive himself. Juan Carlos has a real disease that finally kills him, but Yuddy's illness is psychological, and finds its expression through his narcissistic ego.

The narcissistic ego, Deleuze writes, is 'inseparable not only from a constitutive wound but from the disguises and displacements which are woven

Leslie Cheung – heartbreaker: *Days of Being Wild*

from one side to the other, and constitute its modification. The ego is a mask for other masks, a disguise under other disguises.'[18] In other words, Yuddy's narcissism is a wounded ego, a mask hiding a fractured other, which in essence is 'no more than the pure and empty form of time, separated from its content'.[19] Yuddy suffers from an identity crisis brought on by a Freudian Oedipal complex (the need to connect with his birth mother), and in a sense, expires from this 'pure and empty form of time'. 'Time empty and out of joint, with its rigorous formal and static order, its crushing unity and its irreversible series, is precisely the death instinct,' Deleuze explains.[20] Yuddy's fractured ego is well illustrated in his retelling of the parable of the bird without legs that keeps on flying until it dies – the epiphany being that the bird did not go anywhere because it was already dead to begin with. The character of Yuddy, replete with displays of narcissistic fervour, assumes poignancy in the light of Leslie Cheung's suicide on April Fool's Day 2003, if we were to regard the role as Leslie's narcissistic mask, which paradoxically exposes his troubled ego rather than hides it.

Such is Wong's skill as a director of actors that *Days of Being Wild* plays autonomously with its own dynamics of emotional characterisations even as he is borrowing the characters and situations of *Heartbreak Tango*. Wong has probably borrowed from other literary sources as well, most notably Japanese novelist Haruki Murakami, whose novel *Norwegian Wood* features a male protagonist recollecting an affair from his youth with a woman vulnerable to nervous breakdowns, somewhat like Maggie Cheung's So Lai-chen. The novel's hero searches into his memory and dreads forgetting the most important thing: 'The sad truth is that what I could recall in 5 seconds all too soon needed 10, then 30, then a full minute … ' This line, and the conceit of memory and forgetting, is implicitly evoked in Yuddy, who cannot forget what he wants to forget, namely the affair with So Lai-chen and the 'one minute' of their relationship that is impressed for ever in his mind.[21]

Wong reinterprets *Heartbreak Tango* according to the emotional drives of his actors. Leslie/Yuddy dances the heartbreak tango, metaphorically speaking, with So Lai-chen and Lulu, just as Juan Carlos dances it with Nené and Mabel. The women are forever touched by Yuddy/Juan Carlos, but while Puig provides a social context, setting his protagonists in 'a gossipy and

nauseatingly envious town', Wong's characters are like zombies moving
around somnambulistically in a subtropical urban landscape, abandoned to
the elements by a perfidious lover (the use of the Latin American standard
'Perfidia' is, in this regard, an apposite anthem for the women). Lai-chen
and Lulu carry on their affairs in a 'psychomantic' fashion, because Yuddy is
already dead to begin with (the more animated Lulu temporarily revives
him, but this is superficial, as he fundamentally has no interest in her).
Once jilted, their affairs with Yuddy become affairs of the soul. Like Juan
Carlos, Yuddy has entered the realm of the sublime, but while Juan Carlos
may rest in peace finding niches in the hearts and minds of the women who
loved him, Yuddy finds no such repose: 'I don't know how many more
women I'll love in my life, and I won't know which one I'll truly love on the
day I die' (the insertion of 'Perfidia' at this point becomes an ironic personal lament).

Juan Carlos's friendship with Pancho is mirrored in Leslie/Yuddy's
friendship with Jacky Cheung and Andy Lau, but here Wong has emended on

Carina Lau, good-time girl in love: *Days of Being Wild*

these relationships: Andy's and Jacky's characters are much more evocative. Jacky Cheung in fact gives a purely emotional performance that is plumbed from something deep inside, his face engraved with the pain and sickness of the longing for love. It is a great performance that leaves its impression on the audience long after the film has finished. Cheung's acting style clearly derives from the Method school when contrasted with Andy Lau's approach. Wong instructed Lau to give a Bressonian performance, removing all expression from his face, and concentrating emotion inside instead of letting it burst out. It is an intimate and inward performance, which characterises the tone of the film.

As for the women, Maggie Cheung and Carina Lau perfectly capture the touching qualities of women haunted by Yuddy's Narcissus. Cheung gives the more subtle performance, which becomes more evocative in the light of Cheung's latter rendition of the same character in *In the Mood for Love*, but even Carina Lau, whose character is more flamboyant, manages to give a subdued performance, suggesting a depth of character that has not been plumbed by any other director (with the exception of Tony Au, for whom Lau gave a mature rendition of a kept woman in the 1989 release *I Am Sorry*, capturing both the flamboyance and depth of her character in *Days of Being Wild*). All the actors are keyed into a uniform tone of inner emotion, which only shows that the characters they play are essentially Wong's own creations, and, perhaps, apart from Leslie/Yuddy's primal obsession and death instinct (which, in hindsight, belong more to Leslie's psychological condition), that their inwardness reflects the director's fundamentally shy nature.

Wong comes as close as anyone yet to mastering the structure of Puig's novel in its intricate linkage of seemingly disparate and unrelated elements. He achieves this through a combination of monologic dialogue and allowing the characters to have their own emotional space without a common thread of a plot structure:

> Since few people will pay any attention to the method of telling a story, I wanted to change a certain attitude about structure, making it so that the audience wouldn't guess what will happen next. I feel that surprise is very important.[22]

That Wong, still then a relative newcomer, was able to bring off a film shaped entirely by its characters rather than by the story, and with the complicity of major stars (already a sign of the director's ability to exert total control) makes *Days of Being Wild* an extraordinary achievement. The material may be frail but Wong has produced cinema out of it, and within his own cultural and aesthetic norms. Puig's influence has rubbed off on Wong in an unexpectedly inverse way, since his stories were a product of his love of cinema, his novels being peppered with references to classic Hollywood movies, and the jumbled, elliptical way that he constructs his conversations between characters representing not so much stream of consciousness as the staccato rhythm of cinematic jump-cuts.

Though Wong is rightly the auteur of *Days of Being Wild*, the creative input of his collaborators cannot be ignored. Here, as in *As Tears Go By*, William Chang exerts a crucial creative role as production designer. Chang's meticulous design foregrounds the 1960s, both in the Hong Kong and Philippines scenes, bringing the period to reality (or as close either to Wong's or Chang's own memory of it) in front of the audience's eyes. The production design renders a coherence to the film that is apparently lacking in the plot. This time around, Chang's role did not extend into the editing process – this honour was given to Patrick Tam, Wong's mentor from his early days as a scriptwriter, although initially, according to Tam, Chang did cut a few sequences that Wong was apparently unhappy with and he asked Tam to look at it. 'Chang's cut imposed a style or a certain something on the material but it didn't naturally grow from the material,' Tam recalls.[23] Hence, Tam went to work on cutting the picture, but his contribution was to go further: he was ultimately responsible for creating an order out of chaos.[24]

'Wong customarily is not fond of breaking down his scripts into preordained and detailed shots, unlike directors like Hitchcock or Bresson, who would then go on to shoot the script. He would not have a preconceived design or *mise en scène* on the set. He liked to improvise', Tam says.[25] This style of working was particularly suited to Chris Doyle, who was introduced to Wong by Tam.[26] *Days of Being Wild* marks the first collaboration between Wong and Doyle, but according to Tam, Wong was at first exasperated by Doyle's methods. 'I can't control him', Wong would complain to Tam, who replied that he could find nothing wrong with Doyle's photography.[27] But after *Days of Being Wild*, Wong asked Doyle to work with him again: both men were able to operate on the same wavelength and settled into an amicable professional relationship that continues today.

Tam had to sort out the miles of footage that Doyle had shot, based on Wong's script-free style of shooting every scene from all conceivable angles. As Tam sees it, his contribution to the film lies in the opening and the final shots. In the absence of a shooting script or even a complete screenplay (Tam worked only from a synopsis), it was left to him to select the shots of the opening scene where the camera follows Yuddy walking into the foyer of the football stadium and his encounter with So Lai-chen:

> Yuddy is a ruthless kind of man, very dynamic, full of energy. When chasing after girls, he would be direct, straightforward. Therefore right from the opening, that is what you see – no playing around. Which means that I was helping him to structure the film, to break the shots down.[28]

As for the final scene featuring an uninterrupted take of Tony Leung Chiu-wai sitting on his bed in a garret manicuring his fingernails, then getting up to put on his jacket, retrieving a large wad of cash from the table and putting it into his breast pocket, along with a pack of cards that he slips into his vest pocket, folding the handkerchief, and finally combing his hair before switching off the light and going out, Tam says that originally the scene was to play like a trailer announcing Tony Leung Chiu-wai as the star of the next episode. As it stands now, the scene is an integral part of the film, which was Tam's idea. He explains:

> Structurally, it changes the film. The scene is unrelated to all that has happened before and it seems that all the characters were really preparing the stage for Tony Leung to appear. They were like a prologue. This is a very daring touch, and I must say, I draw a lot of satisfaction from it. I synched the whole sequence to the music of Xavier Cugat,[29] and it worked perfectly. He [Wong] liked it, and left it like that.[30]

Tony Leung Chiu-wai's appearance may not be quite the final epiphany of the film, but it matches the inherent mood and Ah Fei syndrome – the syndrome of the self-absorbed, lone individual, charismatic with brilliantined hair and beautiful face, recalling the handsome young men who appear as elusive figures of memory in Puig's novels (usually in the minds of women); or he could be Yuddy's doppelgänger in a lost detective mystery by Borges. Whatever, his presence in *Days of Being Wild* is scintillating, a beacon shining in an almost mythical light. Tony Leung himself believes that this is his greatest performance, and there are many who concur.

Leung appears on screen for all of three minutes and did everything he needed to do to make his performance great, acting with his face and his body, sitting down, getting up, putting things in his pocket, combing his hair, flicking a cigarette, walking off. I would say, however, that the greatness possibly stems from the potential that this character generates, a potential that can never be fulfilled, and that what we have now, what we do see, must be treasured for ever. Episode Two of *Days of Being Wild* is one of the world's great lost movies, and herein lies the heartbreak that is permanently etched on this final scene.

Four
Space–Time Tango: *Chungking Express* (1994)

Refitting Space–Time

The box-office failure of *Days of Being Wild* was a disaster for its production company In-Gear and thus a setback for Wong, finally costing him the second episode of his diptych. While Wong was forced to forgo his project, he was at least consoled by the critical reception of *Days of Being Wild*, which applauded the appearance of a major film-maker. Wong had built up his credentials and contacts to the point that they counted for something despite the failure of his film. He had acquired not only a deserved reputation as a hot new young director but also a certain toughness of spirit (despite his perceived shyness or the softness detectable in his films), insofar as he was able to recover quickly from the setback of leaving *Days of Being Wild* an uncompleted work, or at most a half-fulfilled project.

With the backing and help of Jeff Lau, a fellow partner in In-Gear and a director of surefire hits in the form of quicksilver comedies and action movies, whose status within the industry was far stronger than Wong's at this time (following the huge commercial successes of his Stephen Chow comedy, *All for the Winner* [1990]), Wong left In-Gear to establish his own production company, which he named Jet Tone. He immediately set to work on his next project, involving yet again a major reworking of a novel, this time a classic martial arts novel, Jin Yong's *Shediao Yingxiong Zhuan*, popularly known in English as *The Eagle Shooting Heroes*.[1]

The project was born against a backdrop of the re-emergence of the *wuxia* genre following the success of Tsui Hark's *Swordsman* (also adapted from a Jin Yong novel) in 1990. Wong wrote an entirely original screenplay, using nothing from his source except two or three of its characters, whose back stories he completely invented. He also invented six or seven more characters, interlinked by separate back stories, a device he had used in

Days of Being Wild, but which he would push to the extreme in this new project. He started to shoot his film, entitled *Ashes of Time*, in 1992 as the new *wuxia* cycle was reaching its peak.

Once again, he was able to assemble a cast of big-name stars: Leslie Cheung, Jacky Cheung, Maggie Cheung, Carina Lau and Tony Leung Chiu-wai, all of whom had worked with Wong on *Days of Being Wild*, along with actors he would be working with for the first time, including Tony Leung Ka-fai, Brigitte Lin and Charlie Young. The budget was comparable with *Days of Being Wild*. A period martial arts movie set in old China, *Ashes of Time* posed certain problems for Wong in maintaining his own post-modern aesthetic standards while ensuring that the details in sets, costumes and locations still carried period authenticity. The movie was shot on location in the deserts of China, with the interiors shot in Hong Kong, but although Wong worked at his customary studied pace (the film was a work in progress throughout two years), the pressures of executing a major production so soon after the financial failure of *Days of Being Wild* must have been felt by the director and his crew (by now a repertory company comprising production designer William Chang, director of photography Christopher Doyle, assistant director Johnnie Kong, producer Jacky Pang, and others).

Wong's attention on the film was deflected by having to organise his shoot around the conflicting schedules of his stars, and by his participation in another project that his partner Jeff Lau was directing, *Dongcheng Xijiu*, a parody of *The Eagle Shooting Heroes*, meant by Lau and Wong (who wrote the script together) as a companion piece to *Ashes of Time*. Both films were shot back to back, and used many of the same actors, but while Lau worked very quickly and completed his film in no time, Wong was still working on his film when *Dongcheng Xijiu* was the Chinese New Year attraction in 1993 (*Ashes of Time* was released more than a year later, in September 1994).

Wong also had another project that interrupted the process of completing *Ashes of Time*: namely, *Chungking Express*. The legend of *Chungking Express* is that Wong shot it in under two months during a break in the editing of *Ashes of Time*.[2] Wong likened *Chungking Express* to a film made by students who had just graduated from film school, using the most simple equipment, relying on nothing more than natural light and the documentary circumstances of shooting a low-budget movie. The budget for the film was HK$15 million: Wong stressed that after the rigours of working on two big-budget movies, making *Chungking Express* was like returning to his youth.[3]

That the film feels like a frolicsome adventure is accentuated by the sense that it was shot hurriedly and spontaneously, synchronised to the 'can do' beat of Hong Kong and its film industry. Incredibly for Wong, it was finished quickly and released some two months ahead of *Ashes of Time*. Hence, while *Ashes of Time* is Wong's third movie in the production chronology, it was the fourth film to be released. For this reason, as well as the fact that it is quite literally interlarded between *Days of Being Wild* and *Ashes of Time*, this chapter is devoted to *Chungking Express*. Wong might have intended the film as a relaxing diversion before leading his audience to his next and most demanding work, *Ashes of Time* (which will be discussed in the next chapter), but it is by no means an intermediate or minor work.

Unlike the two films that immediately preceded and succeeded it, *Chungking Express* is not a period film, and it differs from *As Tears Go By* in that it does not fall as neatly into the niche either of a contemporary gangster movie or a contemporary love story. *Chungking Express* is far more quantified in its generic content: a sign of Wong's increasing confidence in creating the kinds of permutations in genre he had sought to do from the very start. It tells two stories that are independent of each other (though Wong inserts into the first episode cameos of the characters who appear in the second).[4]

The main characters are cops (Takeshi Kaneshiro and Tony Leung Chiu-wai), a mysterious lady in a blonde wig (Brigitte Lin) and two kooky women (Faye Wong's sandwich and kitchen hand and Valerie Chow's air hostess). These character descriptions conjure up a variety of genres: cops and robbers, detective noir mystery (the episodes in the first story featuring Brigitte Lin and Takeshi Kaneshiro), comedy and romance (the episodes in the second story featuring Tony Leung and Faye Wong). Wong prefers to call both stories 'single love stories' about people in the city who share the common trait of being unable to channel their feelings to suitable partners:

Tony Leung pours out his feelings to a bar of soap, Faye Wong steals into Tony's apartment and moves things around and that's how she satisfies her feelings, Takeshi Kaneshiro faces a can of pineapples. They project their emotions onto other things. Only Brigitte Lin's character doesn't have feelings. She works non-stop; survival is more important to her. She's like a wild beast let loose in the jungle of Chungking Mansion.[5]

'The jungle of Chungking Mansion' is a reference to the film's Chinese title 'Chongqing Senlin', which translates as 'Chungking Jungle', or alternatively, 'Chungking Forest', denoting the building in Tsimshatsui where the first episode is chiefly set, a hub of small business and criminal activities and also a source of cheap hotel rooms well known to travellers and backpackers. The English title, 'Chungking Express', contains other significations that I will discuss below, but it also serves to mark the division of the film into two episodes: 'Chungking' denoting the first episode, which takes place chiefly in Chungking Mansion, and 'Express' designating the second episode, which pivots around 'Midnight Express', a well-known fast-food outlet located in Lan Kwai Fong in Central, a ferry ride across Victoria Harbour from Tsimshatsui.

Wong's chief inspiration for *Chungking Express* was a short story entitled 'On Seeing the 100% Perfect Girl One Beautiful April Morning' by the Japanese novelist Haruki Murakami. The story is about the mutability of perceptions, and begins with the sentence, 'One fine April morning, I passed my 100% woman on a Harajuku back street'.[6] *Chungking Express* similarly begins with a chance encounter, which becomes a motif in the first episode: Kaneshiro's cop jostles past Brigitte Lin's blonde during a typical cop and robber chase in Chungking Mansion. Reusing the time motif that he had developed in *Days of Being Wild*, Wong cuts to a shot of a clock displaying the date Friday 28 April, as the minute slot shifts to 9.00 p.m. 'In fifty-seven hours, I will fall in love with this woman,' Kaneshiro's lovesick cop intones, retrospectively, in the first-person monologic style that has now become a Wong Kar-wai trademark, but which could also be a continuation of the first-person narrative in Murakami's story. The author's influence on Wong is therefore exerted in two ways: first, in the monologues that reflect the conversational style of the author, and second, in the narrative as a recounting of memory.

The cop eventually meets the blonde in a bar, without either of them being aware of their previous encounter. They strike up a conversation (the woman reluctantly so), and end up in a hotel room. But the vicissitudes of the chance encounter are immediately obvious: she is fast asleep in bed, while he watches old Cantonese movies on late-night TV and stuffs himself with Chef's Salad and French fries.

Wong develops the theme of chimerical relationships with the same evanescence displayed in Murakami's short story. People's lives just touch but never interpenetrate (maybe they do not even touch but just brush past, mere possibilities, foregone opportunities to connect, impermanence). Like Murakami, Wong injects a magical element into everyday life but with a sense of fatal consequences. Like Murakami, he invokes icons from popular culture to suggest the part that memory plays. The casting of Brigitte Lin as the bewigged lady in dark glasses is a conscious raising of her image as a cinematic icon, famous since the 1970s when Wong was a teenager probably just about to enter high school. In *Chungking Express*, the iconic image of Brigitte Lin, whose persona in her early career was that of a beautiful teenager on the verge of womanhood, is suggestive of a figure in another Murakami short story, 'The Girl from Ipanema 1963/1982'. 'The Girl from Ipanema', the title of a popular song from the 1960s, first reminds the narrator of the corridors of his high school, which in turn reminds him of a salad 'consisting of lettuce, tomato, cucumber, green pepper, asparagus, onion and pink Thousand Island dressing', and this in turn brings to mind a girl he used to know, 'confined in an image and floating in the sea of time'. The preponderance of salad in *Chungking Express* is a function of Wong's memory, linked to the iconic presence of Brigitte Lin (in the second episode, it is associated with Faye Wong, whose presence is equally iconic but without the mystique, as she is much younger than either Lin or Wong). But it is also the symbol for hunger – a hunger that arises from the longing for love, a theme that *Chungking Express* revives from *Days of Being Wild*: here, it is not so much unrequited love as lost love.

The other thread that links *Chungking Express* with *Days of Being Wild* is the structure of the diptych. Sadly, Wong was unable to realise the second part of the earlier film, but *Chungking Express* presents a perfect diptych of two single love stories. In this regard, the film is very much a work in its own right, the sweet fruition of an experiment that Wong was unable to complete with *Days of Being Wild*. In making *Chungking Express*, Wong said that he wanted to 'experiment with shooting two crisscrossing stories in one movie', developing the narratives as he went along, 'like a road movie'.[7] Correspondingly, therefore, *Chungking Express* could also be described as an experimental road movie, its experimental nature verified both by its style (a reliance on 'documentary' techniques such as hand-held camera, available lighting, in-camera effects) and the fractured narrative, creating a sense of disorientation in the viewer; except that the kind of disorientation that results from Wong's film comes from what Noël Burch, in *Theory of Film Practice* (first published in French in 1969), predicted would 'form the substance of the cinema of the future', when *découpage* 'in the limited sense of breaking a narrative down into scenes will no longer be meaningful to the real filmmaker ... and will cease to be experimental and purely theoretical and come into its own in actual film practice'.[8]

Chungking Express embodies this actual film practice, in which the formal autonomy of film is used organically by the director to illustrate, in Burch's words, 'a consistent relationship between a film's spatial and temporal articulations and its narrative content, formal structure determining narrative structure as much as vice versa'.[9]

Chungking Space, Express Time

In the paragraphs below, I will seek to demonstrate how *Chungking Express* is a model of post-modern film practice through Wong's orchestrations of spatio-temporal articulations. We might start with the title, 'Chungking Express', in which 'Chungking' is space, and 'Express' is time. 'Chungking Express' is a homogenising metaphor that brings together mutually incompatible concepts. Space in the film is an internal world symbolised by the claustrophobic setting of Chungking Mansion, while time is an external near-abstract world represented by clocks but actualised by the expiry dates on food cans and mock boarding passes drawn on serviettes.

Wong's space is not timeless, but rather it vibrates with a certain philosophical and psychological essence of time, best defined in the French term *durée*, as developed by Henri Bergson.[10] On one level, *durée* means time that passes and continues, and on another level, it refers to time that is associated with consciousness and memory. *Durée* is lived time, the human experience in all its permutations. There is internal or human durée that passes into external space, which then becomes a receptacle of memory. In terms of the film, *durée* is like a tango in which abstract movement (time) dances a compact with space. Space itself can only attain its wholeness by being lived in. Chungking Mansion is a virtual dimension of memory. Its space is a vivid time-filled (hence human and psychological) entity.

As noted before, the title 'Chungking Express' also stands for Tsimshatsui and Central – the spatio-geographical complexes through which time and memory will pass – two geographical locations that Wong had always wanted to film. In Central, apart from the location of the Midnight Express, Wong focuses on the area of the pedestrian escalator from Cochrane Road to the Mid-Levels. Tsimshatsui is delineated by Chungking Mansion. Wong grew up in Tsimshatsui, and it is a locality that he obviously knows well: 'It is a place where the Chinese and the foreigners mix and where there are many distinguishing features of Hong Kong society.'[11] The Mansion represents the multicultural face of Hong Kong, a global village resounding with exotic sounds and languages, and, in Wong's eyes, the real emblem of Hong Kong. The idea of *durée* is present in the reality of the multicultural human experience manifested in the spatial dimension of Chungking Mansion.

Durée is also present in the soundtrack. Wong's ear for foreign sounds extends to his choice of popular songs by artists who have passed on into the world of pop folklore: The Mamas and the Papas' 'California Dreamin'', Dinah Washington's 'What a Difference a Day Makes' and Dennis Brown's reggae-beat 'Things in Life'. Also significant are the snatches of 'Bollywood' soundtracks and Cantonese opera films on late-night TV. This eclectic soundtrack functions as a temporal denomination *over* space. The songs achieve the purpose of rending our senses in our spatial recognition of Tsimshatsui or the Midnight Express. When we hear 'California Dreamin'',

'What a Difference a Day Makes' and Dennis Brown crooning the first two lines of 'Things in Life' ('It's not every day we're gonna be the same way, there must be a change somehow'), we initially feel a note of dislocation before our senses settle down to recognise the space that is associated with a particular song ('California Dreamin'' with the Midnight Express, 'Things in Life' with the popular Bottoms Up bar where Wong shot his bar scenes, etc.).

Space and time appear to be in opposition to each other, but in fact, the songs, the foreign languages of the Mansion and the geography of the locations (Tsimshatsui and Central) work on a purely formal level as texts imparting disparate unities to form one indivisible unity. The title 'Chungking Express' is a deliberate obfuscation of space, imparting the illusion of Tsimshatsui and Central as a unitary city, a whole city. The film's worldwide popularity suggests that audiences who have never been to Hong Kong can legitimately view its play with space and time as an inseparable element of Wong's post-modern style. However, the international version of the film differs to the one shown in Hong Kong. *Chungking Express* was the first of Wong's films to be distributed internationally, having captivated Quentin Tarantino, whose company Rolling Thunder bought the international distribution rights. The worldwide version is longer and contains more scenes in Chungking Mansion of Brigitte Lin setting up her drug deal with a group of Indians, accompanied on the soundtrack by a typical Bollywood song and fragments of dialogue from what must be a Bollywood movie. Later, when Lin is betrayed, there is an extended scene in which she kidnaps a young girl in order to extract information from her father on the whereabouts of her would-be traffickers. A few scenes are reordered or trimmed from the Hong Kong version.

The international version of the film has a more abstract sense of Hong Kong space. To foreign audiences, Chungking Mansion and Midnight Express, Tsimshatsui and Central might as well be only a stone's throw away from each other. The distance between Tsimshatsui and Central, divided by the Victoria Harbour, would of course be apparent to old Hong Kong hands. The Hong Kong version of the film contains a scene in which Takeshi Kaneshiro runs to the Star Ferry and crosses the harbour, as we hear his monologue about buying thirty cans of pineapple with the expiry date of 1

May ('If she doesn't come back, our love will expire'). The deletion of this scene in the international version (the monologue is moved to an extended scene inside the convenience store where Kaneshiro buys his cans of pineapples) further strengthens the illusion of space as one integrated block: Chungking Express as a solid geographical fixture. Yet, the essence of durée, psychologically denoted by the songs, urges the audience to see and think otherwise.

The film's finest expression of *durée* as time and spatial articulations determined by psychological nuances and memory is the sequence that starts the second episode right at the point where the chance encounter motif is recalled: Kaneshiro collides with Faye Wong (ostensibly another '100% girl') while ordering food at the Midnight Express, and Wong freezes the image of their accidental collision. On the soundtrack, Kaneshiro recounts: 'We were just 0.01 of a millimetre from each other. I know nothing about her. Six hours later, she would fall in love with another man.' The scene fades out as 'California Dreamin'' bursts out. Fade in to Tony Leung's cop-on-the-beat signing off the shift roster. He walks straight up to the camera (the off-screen space of Midnight Express), takes off his cap and orders a Chef's Salad. Cut to Faye Wong. She is wearing a black sleeveless T-shirt. 'California Dreamin'' is blazing in real time. The scene takes place in real time, keeping in beat to the song without a cut, the dialogue as follows:

FAYE: Eat here or take away?

TONY: Take away. Are you new here? Haven't seen you before.

(Faye nods her head, her body swaying left and right in rhythm to the music)

TONY: Do you like your music loud?

FAYE: The louder the better. That way, you don't have to think.

TONY: Don't you like thinking?

(Faye shakes her head in time to the music)

TONY: What do you like then?

FAYE: Dunno. I'll tell you when I've thought about it.

Cut to a close-up of Tony's face in profile:

FAYE: What about you?

'California Dreamin'', T-shirts and jump-cuts add up to time and spatial articulations in
Chungking Express (above, opposite and overleaf)

Cut to a close-up of Tony's hand gesturing for her to come closer. Jump-cut to a close-up of their faces, both in profile, entering from frame left and right respectively. He whispers: 'Chef's Salad.' Cut to a medium shot (as before) as Faye responds with a cry of disappointment and Tony walks away with his salad. The camera's gaze remains on Faye, swaying to the music, which has followed the scene in real time. The flow of the music and the image is suddenly interrupted with a jump-cut, like a minor electric recharge. Now we see Faye wearing a lime-green short-sleeved blouse and apron. 'California Dreamin'' is still blazing on the soundtrack, but the time has apparently shifted, and the space has switched to a closer shot of Faye really dancing to the music behind the counter, her hands swinging up and down holding the ketchup. She walks to the kitchen as the boss comes out. He switches off the tape, and there's a cut to Tony who talks to the boss, placing one order of Chef's Salad.

Time is matched to the change of shirts that Faye is wearing. In the preceding scene in the series, she wears a black T-shirt, and in the succeeding one, a lime-green blouse. There are at least two more changes of shirts denoting two more changes of time in the series between Tony Leung and Faye Wong in the Midnight Express. Here, Wong Kar-wai is really expanding in time and space, as only a film director can, Murakami's concept of a relationship by chance encounter and the role of memory. The other two occasions are denoted by a white T-shirt with a black heart festoon, and a white dotted T-shirt.

In the same scene where Faye wears the white T-shirt with black heart time, Tony walks up to the camera exactly as in the introductory shots when the sequence began, right down to taking his cap off – a repetition that is different because it is varied by what Faye wears, and by what Tony orders: this time fish and chips rather than Chef's Salad (following the boss's suggestion to give his girlfriend, who supposedly likes salad, more variety). The scene repeats the essence of the Tony–Faye chance encounter. It is shot from Faye's subjective point of view. In fact, the whole series of shots not only marks the duration of time by what Faye wears but is virtually seen entirely from her perspective. When Tony walks directly up to the camera, his handsome face is completely arresting and we the viewers are quite literally put in Faye Wong's position: our hearts melt with hers, we fancy what she fancies and we share her sense of anxiety and curiosity when Tony now orders fish and chips.

The spatial articulations of the scene are such that they describe Faye's trepidation: she is cleaning a glass wall, from where we see a blurred image of Tony standing by the counter, and she slowly wipes the glass (or the image). Cut to Tony in focus from behind the glass wall; he's stealing a glance at Faye (at us). Cut to Faye, still cleaning, but this time in front of the kitchen porthole, and now wearing a white dotted T-shirt; we are looking through the porthole at Tony from Faye's perspective, although she is actually facing the camera – a dynamic repetition in asymmetrical space emphasised by the recurring rhythm of Faye wiping and cleaning, different spaces in different times. Gilles Deleuze argues that 'the heart is the amorous organ of repetition',[12] and the repetition that occurs in this sequence can be distinguished in terms of psychological and other dimensions of difference. We now learn that Tony's girlfriend has deserted him. 'Since there are so many choices in food, she now wants a change of boyfriends. I should have stuck with Chef's Salad,' Tony says, Faye listening on as she seemingly busies herself cleaning. Tony, looking a bit sad, orders only a coffee.

As Tony drinks his coffee, Wong cuts to a night-time shot of an aeroplane taking off. Tony intones: 'Every plane has a hostess one would like to seduce. Last year, I successfully seduced one at 25,000 feet above the ground.' In Tony's flashback, we are in his apartment: he lies on the bed in the foreground playing with a toy aeroplane, while the air hostess (Valerie Chow) stands by the kitchen door in a bra and skirt, drinking a can of beer; Dinah Washington is singing 'What a Difference a Day Makes'. Space too makes a difference. Tony flies his toy aeroplane to connect with Valerie, and the camera, hand-held with canted angles and pans from left to right to left, follows the couple from one space of the apartment to another in their spontaneous love foreplay, simulating the seduction in the aeroplane at 25,000 feet. When Tony corners Valerie in a passionate kiss, the camera hints at a space in the background: the Mid-Levels elevator is visible beyond the window, with the bed just under it. The flashback scene ends with Tony and Valerie in bed as he manoeuvres his toy aeroplane to make a touch-down on Valerie's naked spine.

The series of shots that I have discussed in some length above is one of the most remarkable displays of cinematic skill in contemporary cinema, as Wong faultlessly masters durée: articulations of space and time, simultaneously bringing into play symbolic meanings and idiosyncratic nuances concerning chance encounters and the vicissitudes of human relationships. Wong might have drawn inspiration from Murakami, but it is impossible to underrate his skill in reabsorbing all his probable sources of influence into his own unique confection of space, time and memory. Besides, Wong proves again how good a director of actors he really is. All four principals give exemplary performances, striking the right notes of heartbreak and whimsy. Brigitte Lin gives a 'blank-face' performance as only she can, and Tony Leung, looking as good in singlet and boxers as he does in uniform, is simply unforgettable (he won the Best Actor Award at the 1995 Hong Kong Film Awards for this role, and quite deservedly so).

Once more, the contributions of Wong's team (production designer William Chang, now supervising the editing, presumably because Patrick Tam was hard at work on *Ashes*[13] and his director of photography, Chris Doyle) must be mentioned. Wong in fact employed two directors of photography on *Chungking Express*: Andrew Lau, who shot the first episode, and Doyle, who shot the second. It is Lau who essentially sets the key for the whole film. For example, Wong returns to the palette of *As Tears Go By* (which was shot by Lau), using mainly blue for the interior shots of Chungking Mansion, and golden sepia for the nightclub. However, here the focus is on movement and speed, an effect achieved through Lau's memorable hand-held camerawork, passing the cue to Doyle for similar effects in the second episode. By reducing colour to a minimum and focusing on light and motion, Lau and Doyle released the kind of energy in film that the Futurists declared should be the aim of art in their manifesto of 1910. Art critic Herbert Read paraphrased this aim well:

> The manifesto of 1910 is a logical document. It begins by declaring that a growing need for *truth* can no longer be satisfied by form and colour as they

have been understood in the past: all things move and run, change rapidly, and this universal dynamism is what the artist should strive to represent. Space no longer exists, or only as an atmosphere within which bodies move and interpenetrate. [14]

The Futurists were attempting to achieve movement on the static canvas. In a certain sense, Doyle and Lau have reverted to the static canvas, as if to return cinema to its origins, reducing movement-images to what Deleuze calls the 'privileged instants' or 'snapshots', in order to re-imagine the sensation of movement.[15] The technique of slow-shutter-speed photography and step-printing creates the recurrent sense of objects in mid-motion or a series of static shots in arrested movement (the strobing slow-motion effect that featured so prominently in *As Tears Go By*, which shows, in retrospect, that this trademark Wong Kar-wai effect was really the work of Andrew Lau, the cameraman on that film). Such a technique creates a distortion of movement, a sense of false speed, which paradoxically has the effect of dynamically heightening velocity.

Chungking Express actually begins by going straight into the movement-image of false speed featuring a false blonde (Brigitte Lin). Speed and movement constitute the prevailing tone of the Chungking Mansion scenes in which Brigitte Lin prepares her troupe of drug-smuggling amateurs. These scenes fulfil the need to tell the story quickly, and do it with remarkable clarity, given that Lau fractures the surface of his images like a cubist painter, thus enhancing the idea that many things are happening at the same time. Like Duchamp's *Nude Descending a Staircase*, Brigitte Lin's character has multiple body parts, metaphorically speaking. In a flurry of limbs, legs and heads, she sets up her team, is double-crossed and exacts revenge. The Futurists' statement 'that motion and light destroy the materiality of bodies'[16] is here put to good use by Wong's cinematographer.

Wong's bodies move and touch and separate, rather than 'interpenetrate'. Kaneshiro and Leung recover from their respective rejections by cultivating an interest in another woman. Yet, in the case of Leung and Faye Wong, it is not clear whether this interest develops into anything deeper (the ending, where Faye watches as Tony refurbishes the Midnight Express, is a bit more hopeful if no less ambiguous than all other Wong films); and it certainly does not in the case of Kaneshiro (or at least, that is the impression). Love is ephemeral, Wong seems to be saying in this film. While this is also the message of the previous films, it is expressed here with a lighter touch: the two cops' reactions to rejection develop from one of morbidity to insouciance, from dejection to a shrug of the shoulders and a smile. Kaneshiro will 'fall in love again in 57 hours'; Leung smiles gently at his old love when she appears with a man on a motorcycle, and he wishes her luck. The Faye Wong character enhances this light-heartedness with her dancing and comical antics, helped by the loud blaring of 'California Dreamin'' and Wong's own rendition of the Cranberries' 'Dreams' (retitled 'The Man of My Dreams' or 'Mengzhong Ren' in Chinese), which are body-swaying, head-nodding and feet-tapping songs in themselves. We too would like to join Faye as she dances and dreams of California.

Finally, as we will move on to discuss *Ashes of Time* in the next chapter, it might be helpful to invoke the thought of that title to ask how *Chungking Express* (already ten years old) and Wong himself will stand up in the journey of time. Wong shows that he is a splendid human instrument of *durée* – time as the speed express, the dynamo of movement, time passing, time continuing, time never coming to an end. Though Takeshi Kaneshiro marks his period of separation from his girlfriend May with tins of pineapples with use-by dates, and Brigitte Lin is given a tin of sardines whose use-by date establishes a deadline by which she must rectify her blunder, time here is not finite but rather material and tangible, because Wong objectifies time: cans of pineapples, a piece of soap, an old wet rag, a shirt, a stuffed toy, a toy aeroplane. Like Proust's *petites madeleines*, these objects are time-carriers transporting the protagonist to a remembrance of things past. Then again, they are like Murakami's skulls in his sci-fi novel *Hard-Boiled Wonderland and the End of the World*. Kaneshiro and Tony talk to these time-objects, somewhat like Murakami's Dreamreader in the novel who looks at skulls and 'reads' their dreams (therefore reading time, which continues).

In *Chungking Express*, time is about human lives, which are subject to permutations and changes: by the first of May, Kaneshiro will be one year older; by the same date, Brigitte Lin may be dead. Such is time. Times passes too in the Midnight Express, marked by changes in Faye's T-shirts. Here, time is something you wear. *Chungking Express*, as the encapsulation, quantification, objectification of time might reach its use-by date at some point in the future. It will then become a skull that future generations of 'dream-readers' will read, and memory will be recovered. *Chungking Express* is an object of time, it is space–time itself, it is something one wears, like Faye's T-shirts – and so far, it has worn well.

Five

Wong's Biographical Histories of Knights Errant: *Ashes of Time* (1994)

A Time to Reinvent

When *Ashes of Time* was finally released in mid-September 1994, Wong, in his most wide-ranging interview up to that time, called it the 'sum-total' of his first three works (the director here counting *Chungking Express* as his third work even though it was his fourth in production).[1] Wong exuded a palpable sense of pride and achievement in his new film. All of his films were about rejection or fear of rejection, he said, and he had pushed this theme as far as it could go in *Ashes of Time*. But the film also marks a new peak in the director's career in other ways. It represents Wong's faculty for survival even after the box-office fiasco of *Days of Being Wild*. *Ashes of Time* was another big-budget production, which took two years to complete. While in the post-production process, he made and released *Chungking Express* in record time, and when work was resumed on *Ashes*,[2] Wong had inevitably compared it with *Chungking*, concluding that it was 'far more substantial', much 'heavier' and 'complex' in scope and depth.[3]

Wong's pride in the film was all the greater, given that he had come under great pressure from his backers (chiefly the Taiwanese production company Scholar Films), who were expecting a 'mass audience' film that could be easily pre-sold overseas.[4] As Wong put it, everybody was expecting to see a martial arts *wuxia* movie, but he had once again confounded expectations, this time claiming that his audience already had a broad idea of his experimental style and method of storytelling from the experience of *Days of Being Wild* and *Chungking Express*, and that they would accept *Ashes of Time* because he had reached a 'mature' stage of his method.[5]

On the surface, the film is different from anything that Wong had done up to this point in his career. His adherence to contemporary genres in his three previous films (gangster, romance melodrama, film noir) makes *Ashes of Time* something of an oddity. It is a period *wuxia* picture, and, as such, falls into the category of a historicist genre entailing quite different frames of reference. Historicism as applied to the martial arts genre is the overall history of knight-errantry and the martial arts in literature and cinema. Conventions established through long historical practice and development are carried on from the past to the present and into the future; one such convention that is characteristic of the genre is history itself.

Historicism points not only to the genre's preoccupation with a mythic history, it also denotes the historical limitations of the genre. For example, Wong was compelled to make a period movie with characters dressed in ancient costumes, or *guzhuang*, in Chinese (the period of *Ashes of Time* spanning roughly the conjoining northern Song and Jin periods of the 12th century). In the Hong Kong cinema, the *guzhuang* movie (or period drama) is interchangeable with *wuxia*, but it can also exist as a separate genre, its focus being on historical anecdote rather than action: such a genre was widespread in the 1950s and 60s, but fell out of fashion in the 70s and 80s as the *wuxia* and kung fu action genres became more popular.

In the 1990s, a new cycle of *wuxia* movies produced by Tsui Hark, *Swordsman*, *Swordsman II* (1992) and *Swordsman III: The East Is Red* (1993), brought the period format back into fashion. These movies revived the classical myth of the swordsman or knight-errant, but from the perspective of a new generation of film-makers reacting against established norms and consciously working to update the genre to suit the tastes of the late-twentieth-century audience. Tsui's series introduced a post-modern *wuxia* cycle that subverted heroic stereotypes and the roles of male and female protagonists. In *Swordsman II*, for example, the character of Dufang Bubai, or 'Asia the Invincible', fluctuates between genders, the yin (the feminine) and the yang (the masculine), having mastered the secrets of a sacred scroll that allows him/her to become the overlord of the world of martial arts. The sexual ambiguity of Asia the Invincible both threatens the image of male heroism and blurs the roles of good and evil archetypes. Consequently, the ostensible hero-swordsman (played by Jet Li) loses his reason for being according to historicist convention. Asia the Invincible turns out not to be as dark or heartless as the character type suggests (an ex-court eunuch and now prospective tyrant of all China), and he/she sacrifices herself at the end of the film out of love for the male hero.

This androgynous figure, embodied by Brigitte Lin, has become the iconic representation of the post-modern evolution of the genre. So successfully did it strike a chord in the Hong Kong audience that Lin herself was hired for almost every movie of that cycle, playing variants or echoes of the androgynous swordsman/swordswoman, most memorably in Ronny Yu's *The Bride with White Hair* (1993) and, of course, in *Ashes of Time*.

The *Swordsman* series was based on a novel by Jin Yong, an author with a pervasive influence on the cinematic *wuxia* genre, so pervasive that even Wong sought to make a movie from something he had written. As he was working within the mainstream of Hong Kong cinema, Wong probably felt obliged to make a period martial arts *wuxia* movie because it reflected a trend, but he also sought to buck this trend by 'making something from Jin Yong that was different from Jin Yong', as Patrick Tam described it.[6] However, Wong had to observe certain formalities of the genre. First, this was his first excursion into the period format, and he also had to handle action in a fashion that he had never really attempted before, namely huge set pieces with elaborate action choreography involving a squadron of stunt actors and a battery of special effects. He hired Sammo Hung, the well-known actor and master choreographer of the martial arts, to direct the action sequences. In this way, he could fulfil the 'expectations' of a martial arts movie, replete with intricate epic-style action of the sort where a single swordsman is pitted against an army of opponents, which leads to a display of the fantastic feats of swordsmanship that are standard fare in the genre.

Second, Wong had somehow to honour the theme of chivalry that traditionally prescribes the genre as a whole. The *wuxia* movie is embedded in a central historical fantasy revolving around an individualistic hero who delivers the common people from oppression and tyranny, imposes order and brings justice to the nation. The deeds of Chinese knight-errantry were exalted by the historian Sima Qian in his monumental *Shi Ji* (translated into

English by Burton Watson as *Records of the Grand Historian of China*[7], written between 104 and 91 BC during the reign of Han Wudi (the 'Martial Emperor'). *Shi Ji* contains two chapters, *Biographies of Knights Errant (Youxia Liezhuan)* and *Biographies of the Assassins (Cike Liezhuan)*, which are the most comprehensive historical accounts of remarkable personalities who could be broadly described as *xia* (or knights errant) and their feats of chivalry and loyalty in the Warring States and Qin periods. In summary, Sima Qian described *xia* in the following terms:

> They always mean what they say, always accomplish what they set out to do, and always fulfil their promises. They rush to the aid of other men in distress without giving a thought to their own safety. They do not boast of their ability and would be ashamed to brag of their benevolence. [8]

This historical view of *xia* and the theme of chivalry (heroes as Robin Hood figures or as Arthurian knights) constitutes the historicist conception of *wuxia* literature and movies, one largely adhered to by film directors and authors in the modern era (for example, the films of King Hu and Zhang Che, or the novels of Jin Yong, Liang Yusheng and Gu Long). *Ashes of Time*, however, does not deal with the theme of chivalry in quite the sense that Sima Qian described it, although it does have something to say about chivalric behaviour in its depictions of *xia* as lovelorn heroes in the tradition of what Chinese martial arts writers call *yanqing* (romantic love).

There are critics, however, who question whether *Ashes* is a *wuxia* movie at all, in the sense that it is a film about chivalry as defined by Sima Qian. Patrick Tam, for example, claims that the movie 'deals with the love stories of several characters who happen to be knights errant: the public may have a mistaken feeling that it is a *wuxia* movie, but it isn't'.[9] I will argue that while Wong was conscious of making a *wuxia* movie, as with everything he had done up to this point, he was reinterpreting genre on his own terms. Wong was really seeking to re-fashion Jin Yong's novel *The Eagle Shooting Heroes* (also known as *The Legend of the Condor Heroes*) on which he was basing the movie.

Wong was only interested in two characters from the novel, Huang Yaoshi and Ouyang Feng (played respectively by Tony Leung Ka-fai and

Leslie Cheung), whose fearsome *noms de guerre*, Dongxie ('Evil East') and Xidu ('Malicious West'), grace the Chinese title of the film. Wong's intention at first was to turn Dongxie and Xidu into female characters, but when he sought to buy the rights to these names, he discovered that he also had to buy the rights to the whole book and was thus bound by legal propriety to retain the original sex of the two protagonists.[10] As he could not contact the author about his characters' back stories, he invented them himself, with the result that *Ashes of Time* is a complete retelling of *The Eagle Shooting Heroes* before its present form. As Wong himself suggests, the novel begins where the movie ends[11] (although to his critics this is misleading, because his characters bear little resemblance to their originals). Extracting the two characters from the novel, Wong presented the viewer with their back histories, examining the emotional complexes of their more youthful days arising from their tragic affairs or relationships with various women (Carina Lau, Brigitte Lin, Maggie Cheung). Wong also took a third character from the novel, the bedraggled knight-errant Hong Qi (played by Jacky Cheung), known as 'Beigai' or the 'Sovereign of the Northern Beggars', to whom he also confers an entirely original back story.

It is possible to see *Ashes of Time* as an intricate deception, a subtle con job to trick the Jin Yong fan, or all devotees of *wuxia* movies, into thinking that it has anything at all to do with the original novel or with the genre as such. The mainland Chinese Jin Yong scholar Chen Mo writes, 'There is no way, and no need, to compare it with the original novel'.[12] Yet, Wong himself says that his movie is not entirely unrelated to the novel[13] – and this is exactly the stance on which I will base my analysis of the film.

As with *Days of Being Wild* and *Chungking Express*, Wong's narrative style is associated with the structures and sources of novels and genres that he has become fond of, and to my mind, it is infinitely more productive to consider how *Ashes of Time* is related to its ostensible source than to dismiss out of hand any relationship to the novel or its genre. The film is indeed a subtle deception, but one conjured up by Wong's exploitation of the associations with Jin Yong's novel and the historicism of the genre to fashion a tome about time. It can legitimately be seen as both a Jin Yong adaptation (albeit a radical reworking) and a martial arts *wuxia* movie (albeit an uncon-

ventional one) that fits into the pattern of Wong's time motif and his preoccupation with the past and memory. *Ashes of Time* is linked to the three previous films through the time motif, signalled by all their English titles: *As
Tears Go By*, *Days of Being Wild*, *Chungking Express*. But, just from a symbolic
reading of the title 'Ashes of Time' (time as dust and ashes, time lying in
ruins), it seems a much more extreme treatment, a more heartfelt lament of
time than previous works.

Part of the reason may be that it goes further back into the past – a past
determined by the genre itself – whereas in the other movies, the genres
exert a minimal impact on time, history or memory; rather it is Wong's own
memory of the past (the 1960s in *Days of Being Wild*) and his cognition of
time and space in *Chungking Express* and *As Tears Go By* that determine the
structures of those films. By this, I do not mean to imply that Wong did not
exert a creative input into *Ashes of Time*, rather that he saw the period setting
of the *wuxia* movie as an opportunity to rework his obsession with time by
stretching it into an abstract past and into the realm of the historical and the
concept of the *jianghu* (literally 'rivers and lakes': a mythical historical time
and place where knights errant roamed and dispensed their form of justice
and righteousness). Time is associated with history in the abstract. It is a
history of the past and of memory; it is a history of time. Time is that substance that flows from the characters, and, somewhat in the manner of the
ancient grand historian Sima Qian, Wong 'writes' the biographies of his
knights errant, whose deeds he sees as relevant to history. His biographies
rescue forgotten figures from the ashes of time; and the English title works
here as a positive metaphor: time (history) rising from the ashes like a
phoenix.

A Time to Eulogise

The historicism of the genre confers a piquancy to the time motif. Here,
history functions as a teleological process that determines the final nature
of its characters and the course of events, which makes sense of Wong's suggestion that we could see the movie as the beginning of the novel. The film's
association with the novel assumes the dimension of a moral and psychological examination of chivalry. In the novel, Huang Yaoshi and Ouyang

Feng are two ruthless patriarchs and mutual rivals, rather disagreeable characters, and all of a piece with Jin Yong's favoured depictions of despotic elders possessing immense power who let nothing stand in their way. They seek to subdue, if not to kill, the naïve young heroes who may one day surpass them in their martial arts prowess (cf. 'Asia the Invincible' in the *Swordsman* series).

In the film, Huang Yaoshi and Ouyang Feng are depicted as younger men but not as 'evil' or as 'malicious' as their portrayal in the novel. Wong saw them rather as 'selfish' and 'tragic', characterisations modulated to the original depictions in the novel.[14] Thus, watching the movie, we now understand why Huang Yaoshi and Ouyang Feng have become what they are in the novel, which provides only slight clues to their characters' pasts: Huang is a widower with a young daughter, Huang Rong, who lives on a secluded island (his wife having died from the physically exhausting task of committing to paper the obscure secrets of a Daoist martial arts bible that she had memorised while in the last stages of pregnancy), and Ouyang Feng an old bachelor who harbours the secret that his nephew, Ouyang Ke (an obnoxious womaniser who has his eye on Huang Yaoshi's daughter), is really his son. As for Hong Qi (Jacky Cheung), the novel depicts him as a straggly, eccentric beggar and a gastronome (with a huge appetite for the gourmet food cooked by Huang Yaoshi's daughter, to whom he eventually passes on the title of the 'Sovereign of the Northern Beggars' after being treacherously wounded by Ouyang Feng in a duel).

The novel draws a portrait of two ageing and reclusive characters at the peak of their powers, who are caught up in an unending series of events that necessitate their coming out as men of action to dispense punishment or mercy to interconnecting groups of martial arts fighters whose paths cross haphazardly; the movie, however, portrays Huang and Ouyang as younger swordsmen in their prime, but who are descending into premature dotage and are given to melancholic reminiscences and ruminations about memory. Wong's theme of memory and lost love, or, more precisely in this instance, love that has been betrayed, is a determining factor in the characters' behaviour. Huang Yaoshi drinks out of a jug of wine that will erase his memory, because he wants to forget his betrayal of a friend (the blind

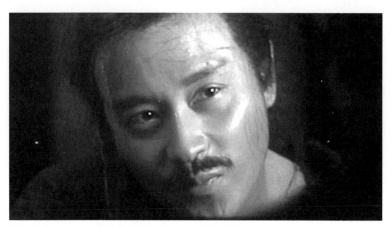

Leslie Cheung, remembered and not forgotten: *Ashes of Time*

swordsman, played by Tony Leung Chiu-wai) with whose wife he had had an affair. Ouyang Feng, for whom the wine was actually intended, finally drinks from it but still remembers his old love, his brother's wife (the Maggie Cheung character). 'The more you seek to forget, the more you remember,' Ouyang says. For him, memory is a joke with an ironic edge: 'It is said that the surest way to lose something is to keep it in your memory.' The wine cannot wipe out Ouyang's memory, but it may just turn it upside down and back to front (Ouyang, as played by Leslie Cheung, is the mirror image of Yuddy in *Days of Being Wild*, who pretends not to remember So Lai-chen when he in fact cannot forget her). Ouyang Feng is the tragic swordsman, an oriental Ethan Edwards (from John Ford's *The Searchers* [1956], the chief cinematic inspiration behind *Ashes of Time*), whose fate it is to wander eternally in memory of a woman he cannot marry.

Wong portrays Ouyang Feng as a cynical swordsman who has withdrawn into the desert after leaving Maggie Cheung in Camel Mountain, his birthplace. He becomes a tavern keeper, acting as a sword-for-hire or as middleman for other swords-for-hire. Ouyang and the desert tavern form the axis of the film. Huang Yaoshi rides in to give him the jug of memory-wiping wine; Brigitte Lin's yin-yang character hires him to kill Huang Yaoshi (because Huang had jilted her); a young woman (Charlie Young) seeks his help to find an avenger who will exact vengeance on those who have killed her brother; Tony Leung's blind swordsman seeks a commission in order to earn cash for his trip back to 'Peach Blossom' land to see the blossoms bloom before he goes completely blind ('Peach Blossom' is the name of his wife: it is she he really wants to see); and Hong Qi drops in to make a name for himself as a killer, loses a finger during a battle (as Charlie Young's anointed avenger) and leaves with his wife (Bai Li) who has followed him to the tavern and who now faithfully continues to follow him as he wanders in the *jianghu*. All the characters are fundamentally old in spirit if not in body. The desert tavern is like a halfway house for characters who are losing memory, losing eyesight, losing fingers, losing brothers and lovers, and losing lives. The tavern, standing at the crossroads of history, is the site of inevitable loss.

It is instructive that Wong should set most of *Ashes of Time* in a wayside tavern. This is an explicit reference to the setting of many *wuxia* movies directed by King Hu and Zhang Che, which identify the tavern as the site of history, where knights errant pass through and leave their mark and perhaps their bodies through death in duels and battles. In the historicist tradition of the genre, the tavern is also the site of the *jianghu*, or a concrete

The desert tavern setting of *Ashes of Time*

Staggered images of blurred action: *Ashes of Time*

manifestation of this abstract space. So far, Wong has observed what I call
the 'formalities' of the genre: the examination of chivalry; the staging of
swordfights; the tavern setting as an allusion in its own right to *wuxia*
movies, as well as a metaphor of the *jianghu*; and, as a concession to the
post-modern evolution of *wuxia* cinema, the inclusion of Brigitte Lin as a
yin-yang character named Murong Yin and Murong Yang. It is now necessary to consider the other equation of *Ashes of Time* that has now passed into

the critical folklore, which is Wong's subversion of the historicist notions of *wuxia*. The view of Wong as a post-modern artist hinges on his tendency to defragment his narratives into clusters of characters and mini-plots, into Puig-like 'episodes', all of which flow into a Borgesian labyrinth. Wong draws on a variety of influences, both cinematic and literary, but once they have passed through his hands, these influences are transformed, becoming tenuous and indiscernible.

If post-modernism itself is subversive, then the underlying truth is that Wong has subverted the genre. As an example, his fight scenes are entirely impressionistic, in the style of the step-printed slow-motion effect that is now one of his trademarks, so fast and furious that we never see any actual fight moves as in a King Hu or a Bruce Lee film. It may even be said that Wong has deliberately obfuscated his fight scenes, giving us only the sensation of a fight: whirling bodies, an occasional close-up of a face in death throes, blurred movements of one against many. The perspectives are flattened, the images a force of the imaginary, or an optical illusion. Yet the impression of ferocity and desperation is maintained and is in keeping with the norms of the genre.

Ackbar Abbas believes that 'the film does not obviously parody or ironize the conventions of the genre. Rather, the implications of the genre are followed through to their catastrophic conclusions.'[15] I would suggest that Wong is providing a running commentary on the genre. Here, we should invoke the idea of Wong's historical sense as a counter-memory. The gist of his historical sense, which is also behind his 'subversion' of narrative structure, is the Foucaldian idea of 'effective history', which deals 'with events in terms of their most unique characteristics, their most acute manifestations. ... The forces operating in history are not controlled by destiny or regulative mechanisms, but respond to haphazard conflicts.'[16] By conforming to the historicist framework of the genre, Wong's post-modern sensibility appears to subvert the genre, but in 'writing' his historical biographies of knights errant, he is providing us with an 'effective history' of human characteristics determined by emotion and memory rather than a grand design of history.

Essentially, Wong critiques two historicist notions: the theme of chivalry and the concept of the *jianghu*. Wong's knights errant pass through the tavern, the *jianghu* site where their intersecting relationships relate to the past, signified by memories of the women they love. The women's haunting presence, whether existing in the minds of the swordsmen or present in reality, symbolises the end of chivalry. The romantic dreams of knight-errantry are diminished by betrayal, jealousy, infidelity or even schizophrenia, in the case of the Brigitte Lin character, whose personality is split into male and

Brigitte Lin lends her iconic presence to *Ashes of Time*

female sides (and who later becomes a mysterious swordswoman known as the 'Defeat-Seeking Loner', practising sword fighting with her own reflection in the water). In this *jianghu*, swordsmen wander for selfish motives. No longer are they knights errant who fight for the ideals of chivalry and justice (perhaps with the sole exception of Hong Qi, who, as an intertitle informs us, would fight a duel with Ouyang Feng years later in the Snow Mountain, resulting in both their deaths).

There is a growing tide of scholarship that views the post-modern martial arts cinema as allegories of Hong Kong and its troubled future regarding China and the 1997 issue.[17] The Hong Kong academic Stephen Ching-kiu Chan sees the end of chivalry in *Ashes of Time* as figurative of Hong Kong's state of mind in the transitional period before its reversion to Chinese sovereignty: 'With *Ashes of Time* we are thrown into a world not of generic heroism, but one where the erosion of all heroic values had just completed its transitional historical course.'[18] The *jianghu* in *Ashes of Time* and other 'postmodern' martial arts movies released around the same period (including Tsui Hark's *Swordsman* series, Tsui's *The Blade* [1995] and the remake of *Dragon Inn* [1993]) is a trope for Hong Kong itself, where 'neither the urge for unification nor the value of coherence can be realized'.[19]

Yet, for all its post-modern, post-colonial qualities in the eyes of scholars such as Stephen Chan, *Ashes of Time* exists as a work that is ultimately rather faithful to the genre and can be appreciated purely on its own terms. Its themes – revenge, chivalry and the wanderlust of *xia* – are consistent with the conventions of the genre. The narrative structure is fragmented, a post-modern trait in itself, but it is also a characteristic of *wuxia* literature. Jin Yong's novel features multitudinous characters, each with their own back story, and narrative episodes seemingly unconnected with each other – and the plot of each episode is constantly interrupted by accounts of swashbuckling adventure. While Wong undoubtedly makes full use of this novelistic convention as a style of his own to critique the genre, he also looks back on it with fondness. The music, for example, recalls the synthesized scores and theme songs of many a TV *wuxia* serial based on epic martial arts novels. Wong's use of montages depicting crowd-combat scenes to open and close the film resembles the opening credit-montages of TV series. Accordingly, the last shot of Leslie Cheung charging at his enemies with his sword as Frankie Chan's electronic music pumps up to a crescendo comes across as a humorous post-modernist take on anachronistic conventions.

Ashes of Time pays homage to the *wuxia* novel. Like most Hong Kong directors, Wong harbours a fondness for the genre derived from memories of his childhood consumption of its novels and movies. This nostalgic, mnemonic quality is evoked in *In the Mood for Love* through his protagonists sharing a fondness for *wuxia* novels, and, on the pretext of writing such novels, deepening their affair of the heart. The presence of the nostalgic element in *Ashes of Time* is its eulogy to the genre and to past masters: Jin Yong, King Hu, John Ford. Wong seems to suggest that any director wishing to reactivate the genre could only do so by keeping the form of the *wuxia* novel and its themes intact. Not for nothing did he reply completely without irony, when asked what was new and fresh about *Ashes of Time*, that he had done 'something traditional, something that was easy to understand and in fact, very plain'.[20] Far from being disingenuous, Wong was rather guiding his interlocutor, and us, towards a certain understanding of the film.

In the final analysis, irrespective of whether Wong was trying to subvert the genre or not, *Ashes of Time* is a triumph of the plastic imagination: an achievement of the teamwork of Wong, production designer William Chang (also a member of the editing team headed by Patrick Tam), director of photography Christopher Doyle, music composer Frankie Chan, costume designer Luk Ha-fong, sound editor Ching Siu-lung and the props department. *Ashes of Time* is Wong's best-made film in that all the departments click. Never before has the *jianghu* looked as fashionably appealing as it does here.

Its inhabitants are dressed in vaguely traditional Chinese costumes that in fact recall the monochromatic creations of those Japanese designers who startled the fashion world in the 1980s (designers like Issey Miyake, who emphasised the movement of the body rather than the body itself, designing clothes with trailing hems and sleeves made out of hemp-like material or distressed fabrics that had been crimpled and pleated). Wong's unwashed and unkempt heroes and heroines would have looked at home on a Paris fashion catwalk. The accent on fabric textures in the characters' costumes is no accident. Textures abound and recur in this film, not only in the clothes, baskets, lanterns and hats, umbrellas and slippers but also in the water, earth and sky – textures created by ripples on water, desert scrubs, craggy cliffs, cloud formations. Everything in this film is an opportunity to use textures, and at every turn our tactile senses are aroused: from the dark, glossy smoothness of a horse's skin to the rough wrinkles on tree bark. Indeed, there are scenes of hands stroking, squeezing and rubbing that have less to do with the narrative and are more concerned with the tactile sensation that the director wants us to feel, a desire that he takes to the extreme, as in the scene where Peach Blossom embraces her horse, and also in the episode where Brigitte Lin's Murong Yin embraces the twisted and gnarled trunk of a tree as if mating with it. Like a textile artist, Wong weaves together the pieces of his narrative with the use of textures.

Visually, the landscape of the *jianghu* is reminiscent of the landscape paintings of John Olsen, the Australian artist who painted a picture of the Australian outback he called *The Land Beyond Time*. This could be a fitting title for Wong's *jianghu*. It is a land that exists only in the imagination and where magical things happen. Christopher Doyle's cinematography conjures up just such a place. Only in the *jianghu* can a person who is both yin

Reflection in a waterhole: *Ashes of Time*

and yang fight his or her own reflection with a sword that yields cascades and torrents out of a placid lake; or a man ride a horse upside down across the landscape (reflected in the water); or defeat an army on horseback by dislodging a cliff with the mere flick of a sword; where Brigitte Lin's Murong Yin can flip a saucer and it becomes a moon.

The empty desert plain where the *jianghu* is located echoes with the same sense of personal isolation as did the empty alleyways and stairways of early Wong Kar-wai films. When Ouyang gazes out at the bare lonely landscape of sand and dust, he sees his own soul. The moving shadows and reflections cast by objects in the natural world create movement where human beings are motionless – most strikingly illustrated in the scenes that take place in Ouyang's cave-like tavern: the basketry of a birdcage whirls against the light, creating moving shadows across the face of Murong Yin as she struggles with her emotions. Similarly, Peach Blossom astride a horse standing motionless in the water hardly moves, but the reflection of the water on her face creates motion in a motionless scene. This contradiction of motion in stillness renders a Zen-like ambience to the film.

The film begins with a quote from a Zen Buddhist canon: 'The flags are still, no wind blows. It is the heart of man that is in tumult.'[21] In fact, visu-

Maggie Cheung pondering the past in *Ashes of Time*

ally, the reverse occurs in the film. When not fighting for their lives, the characters appear subdued, dreamlike, dazed, even drugged. They speak in low monotones. There are many shots of the characters doing nothing but staring into the distance. But the external world is in agitation: the wind blows, flags and banners are seldom still, the water sparkles and moves, the tide heaves and turns. Even the long hair of Huang (often waving in the wind) is put to good use in creating motion. By these means, Wong expresses the inner agitation of man, which can burst into violence, and then, when blood spurts out like a geyser, it sounds like the wind.

The movie sounds different from all three previous Wong films. The score (composed by Frankie Chan, working with Wong for the second time after *Chungking Express*) employs a hybridised style, without recourse to the practice of including the snatched snippets of contemporary pop music that we hear in *As Tears Go By*, *Days of Being Wild* and *Chungking Express* (memorably so in the case of the last two films). The score itself tends to be parodic, but at moments it perfectly heightens the pathos of the characters, most effectively Maggie Cheung's vivid portrayal of the dejected lover in the mode of Hippolyta, one of Baudelaire's 'Damned Women': a foolish, fallen angel, who enlisted 'love in the service of morality' (foreshadowing the housewife

that Cheung will play in *In the Mood for Love*).[22] In her dialogue scene with
Huang Yaoshi, Cheung laments the past ('How wonderful it would be if we
would could go back to the past') as the music drones on effusively, marked
by chromatic alterations that plumb the depths of her despair at every turn.

But finally, the movie sounds different because it contains the most dialogue and monologues (and the most intertitles) of any Wong Kar-wai film.
Wong states that, as a child, his first contact with martial arts novels was
through the radio, and that with *Ashes of Time*, he sought to replicate that
sensation of listening to dialogue by writing as much as he could for the
film: 'The film is one that you can listen to and understand'.[23] *Ashes of Time*
ends with Ouyang Feng deciding to leave the desert. He burns his tavern, the
fire itself suggestive of the burning of time, like the burning of Nené's letters at the end of *Heartbreak Tango*. As the fire blackens and destroys our
memory sensations and the epigrammatic sentences start to dissipate into
ashes, the words break loose, sounded and echoed by the wind before they
disappear into eternity:

> 'How wonderful it would be to go back to the past ...', 'the best way to avoid
> rejection is to reject others first ...', 'memory is the fount of worry ...', 'the
> more you wish to forget ... the more you remember ...', 'the surest way to lose
> something is to keep it in your memory ...', 'man's biggest problem is that he
> remembers too well ... wouldn't it be nice if we could forget everything ... and
> each day would be a new beginning ...'

Six
Pathos Angelical: *Fallen Angels* (1995)

The Eternal Return

Wong's image as the *enfant terrible* of Hong Kong cinema was reaffirmed by the box-office flop of *Ashes of Time*, and the fact that this did not deter him from going ahead immediately with his next production, *Fallen Angels*, another quirky, apparently self-indulgent film after the manner of *Chungking Express*, which was the film that propelled him into international prominence (although it too under-performed at the domestic box office). *Fallen Angels* was released in 1995, a year after *Ashes of Time*, but its origins actually stem from *Chungking Express*: it was the third story that was never made due to the problem of length. Wong now expanded this third story and developed it into another self-contained diptych, so that *Fallen Angels* is both an outgrowth of and a companion piece to *Chungking Express*. Wong was highly conscious of public perceptions that he was repackaging old goods, and when asked what his 'special method' was in extracting something fresh and new out of old materials gave this reply:

> Looks like it's no longer a question of whether or not you are packaging it with anything new but one of re-arranging what's already there and this process is another kind of creativity. Actually, many film stories and genres are used over and over again. Only, one has to figure out when's a good time to re-adjust them and film them so that they are a good fit with modern times. It is human experience to fall into habit, and watching movies is a form of habit. You might feel strange when a plot is taken out of sequence, but when you get used to it, it is no longer a problem. This is how we live.[1]

As Wong conceived it, *Fallen Angels* is clearly a return to the form of *Chungking Express*, but is it obviously the same thing? Wong's oeuvre by now raises the question of repetition, betraying an eternal return to the same themes and images: the habit of human experience. The philosophical question of identity that Deleuze elucidates in *Difference and Repetition* tells us that returning is being, 'but only the being of becoming'. As Deleuze writes: 'The eternal return does not bring back "the same", but returning constitutes the only Same of that which becomes. ... Repetition in the eternal return, therefore, consists in conceiving the same on the basis of the different.'[2]

Ashes of Time was a return to *Days of Being Wild* but was also utterly different; now *Fallen Angels* returns to *Chungking Express* in a fashion that makes them identical twins, but here the sameness rebounds through a mirror with a crack. The director signals early in the film that 'There is a difference' by showing us these very words – the tag line in an IBM commercial – flashing by on a TV screen inside Leon Lai's apartment as Michele Reis busies herself cleaning it. In both *Ashes of Time* and *Fallen Angels*, Wong is both the agent of the eternal return and the agent of difference.

Wong set out to make *Fallen Angels* look different. He underscores the difference by employing new stars for the first time (Leon Lai, Michele Reis, Karen Mok, all of whom give very good performances, as do Takeshi Kaneshiro and Charlie Young, both working with Wong for the second time). There are a lot more colours, and the use of 'supplementary hand-held cameras', as Wong put it (referring to the use of video cameras),[3] but the single most important distinguishing mark is the change of visual perspective. Wong shot the film almost entirely with a super wide-angle 9.8mm lens. He called it the 'standard lens' of the film, and the effect this exerts on the viewer is a distortion of space, conveying a sense of distance in closeness, of being near and yet far away.

This wide-angle perspective is the core of the difference, pushing the film's similarity with *Chungking Express* to the periphery. Like its seemingly identical cousin, *Fallen Angels* is a film about the city, but the way that Wong presents the city, and the title itself, implies that it is a *whole* city rather than the divided space of Kowloon and Hong Kong that *Chungking Express* signifies. Hong Kong is a city of fallen angels, and to the extent that Wong's Hong Kong is a city of the mind, a psychological city, the director's wide-angle perspective implicates the viewer: we are all fallen angels. On the other hand, the enveloping, all-inclusive perspective brings out the theme of identity: in one way or another, we identify with the fallen angels who are Wong's characters. After all, we live in the same city, psychologically speaking, and Wong's idea was to show the relationships of people living in a dense urban environment, where everyone is physically close to each other but mentally apart.[4]

There are five key characters: a professional hitman (Leon Lai), his female agent (Michele Reis), his forgotten ex-girlfriend with dyed blonde hair (Karen Mok), an ex-jailbird mute named He Zhiwu (Takeshi Kaneshiro, on the surface assuming the role of the character with the same name he played in *Chungking Express*) and the woman (Charlie Young) he meets on the street as she's making a phone call and who, upon learning that her lover will soon marry another woman, cries on the mute's shoulder. These fallen angels are innocents who share the condition of having sunk deep into the city's infernal regions, although some retain a certain joy in life and continue to seek happiness. Hence, *Fallen Angels* perfectly complements

Takeshi Kaneshiro – a biker and his angel in *Fallen Angels*

Chungking Express, in that they are the most optimistic of Wong's films, though in fact the former is much darker in tone and more psychological.

One can read biblical inferences into the title: the fall of Adam and Eve and God's curse upon the ground; or a more apocalyptic New Testament vision of angels who left their first estate and descended into the hell of the city, reserved in everlasting chains under darkness awaiting judgment day. There are also close allusions to Jack Kerouac's *Dharma Bums*, and the members of the Serpent Club in Cortázar's novel, *Hopscotch*. Like the protagonists of these two works, the fallen angels are misplaced souls darting around in a city that is both benign and malignant, finding redemption in each other and then forgetting that they have ever met (re-manifesting Wong's theme of memory and time). The fallen angels, the 'Dharma bums', the Serpent Club members scour the streets of different metropolises, guessing that in some part of Los Angeles, San Francisco, Paris or Hong Kong, some day, or some death, or some meeting will show them the key.

The film is essentially composed of various episodes that show the fallen angels as socially isolated creatures, on the brink of madness or mental breakdown. They are the featured players in a number of pathological episodes that mark their characterisations as fallen angels, but as an optimistic take on pathological behaviour, the film is perhaps best seen as a jazzy psychoanalytical jam session. As it opens, the viewer is set up for just such an exercise: the first scene is a two-shot of the meeting between Leon Lai's hitman and his agent Michele Reis in a bar, both characters facing the camera laterally but with a sense of distance between them; Reis is close to the camera, while Lai is positioned well in the background (here the depth-of-field effect of Wong's wide-angle lens allows a distant view of Lai and a close-up of Reis in one striking shot, which captures the essence of two people close to each other, yet distant). Reis's hand is shaking as she brings a cigarette to her mouth and asks, 'Are we still partners?' Lai responds with a monologue:

> We've been partners for 155 weeks. Today's the first time we've sat close to each other. We've maintained a distance because human emotion is difficult to control. The best partners are those who don't let emotion rule their relationship.

Two speaking subjects try to carry on a dialogue, but they communicate not with each other but with us, the viewer. The dialogue between the two characters is phenomenological (one speaks, one hears, and therefore both are), but their communication with each other is psychological – the psychic space between them is the distance emphasised by the camera lens. From the start, Wong poses an open-ended intertextuality between dream and reality, between psychical and physical processes (the theme of conflicting distance and closeness). What follows after this dialogue is possibly a psycho-pathological flashback in the mind of Michele Reis, depicting the nature of her relationship with Lai. Reis goes to her silent client/interlocutor's apartment to clean it up, collects his garbage and brings it back to her own room to 'read' the contents. She also masturbates in his bed. All that Reis does is to communicate psychologically with her 'partner'. If communication is a theme, it is presented through a mental-emotional lens that disorients our sense of time (during her cleaning, Reis rewinds the clock, which shows either that time has stopped or that it is beginning over again). Reis and Lai do not speak to each other directly in the course of this flashback until we return to the scene of their bar meeting about two-thirds into the film, when Lai actually replies to her question, 'Are we still partners?' In everything we have seen before that, the communication between the two protagonists is undertaken through pagers and faxes, through rituals (the cleaning up, the phone messages) and songs (Laurie Anderson's 'Speak My Language' and Shirley Kwan's Canto-pop number 'Forget Him').

Leon Lai's killer is a blank space, an anonymity (and the actor does give the most anonymous-looking performance in a Wong Kar-wai film). He embodies the structural distance of the film. In psycho-linguistic terms, as it is he who delivers the first monologue, which marks the beginning of the narration, he also embodies the experience of emptiness 'at the very origin of narration', in the words of Julia Kristeva, from her analysis of Bakhtin's theory of narration.[5] Lai's monologue is the zero degree of the narration, emphasising distance and non-emotion, and this is another level of difference that distinguishes *Fallen Angels* from *Chungking Express*. Lai reflects Wong Kar-wai the author, who is reading himself vis-à-vis *Chungking Express* and reminding his audience that he is maintaining a distance from the earlier film, although the references will flow fast and loose as *Fallen Angels* unfolds.

Where Fallen Angels Tread

Fallen Angels, like all of Wong's films, is told from the multiple perspectives of its characters, and all of them reflect Wong, the writer and author. The monologic discourses rebound back on Wong, exposing him as perhaps dangerously schizoid, split into several personalities. I am not suggesting that Wong is himself psychotic. If anything, his movies reveal a basically well-balanced and un-neurotic personality. However, I am saying that Wong's poetic language is structurally pathological and deeply ambivalent, and that it is worthwhile examining the *structural* source of his pathology.

This book has sought to study and demonstrate Wong's debt to literature in greater detail than usual, since it is my conviction that he is as much a literary director as a visual one, but in a sense, there is a clash of two artistic personalities: first, the post-modern visual stylist, and second, Wong's skills as a writer with a penchant for poetic, epigrammatic language. No other Hong Kong director uses monologue and dialogue in the same way as Wong, and none are able to write and direct as he can. In truth, Wong's monologic discourses put him only alongside Godard as a director who reconciles literature with cinema, though he has modestly said that his lines are not as poetic as Godard's.[6]

Wong's narrative model is very much in the Godardian mould of monologue, dialogue, and extratextual quotes from a variety of literary or semi-literary sources – novels, songs, poetry, films. His narratives, like Godard's, are imitations of monologic discourse: stuttered, fragmented, with abrupt transitions and changes, a series of misalliances – hence a structural pathology of narrative. This structural tendency of pathology, which Wong also utilises to characterise his human protagonists, has its roots in the polyphonic carnivalesque discourse of the novel that Bakhtin brought to attention in his study of Rabelais. Wong's own polyphonic style of writing (which includes not only the writing of dialogue and monologues but also the 'writing' of the film as a totality, on the principle of film as a language) is highly carnivalesque, of a kind that incorporates a Menippean discourse (after the satirical style of the ancient Greek philosopher Menippus), a style that is both comic and tragic, as Kristeva informs us:

> Pathological states of the soul, such as madness, split personalities, daydreams, dreams and death, become part of the narrative. According to Bakhtin, these elements have more structural than thematic significance; they destroy man's epic and tragic unity as well as his belief in identity and causality; they indicate that he has lost his totality and no longer coincides with himself. At the same time they often appear as an exploration of language and writing ... Menippean discourse tends towards the scandalous and eccentric in language. The 'inopportune' expression, with its cynical frankness, its desecration of the sacred and its attack on etiquette, is quite characteristic.[7]

Judging by the pathological states of his characters' souls, Wong's Menippean discourse has been clear from the start. From *As Tears Go By* to *Days of Being Wild* to *Ashes of Time*, his characters are chronically pathological. Fly (Jacky Cheung) in *As Tears Go By* is practically on the verge of madness; Yuddy has an Oedipal complex that leads him to persistent womanising in *Days of Being Wild*; Brigitte Lin is a split yin-yang personality in *Ashes of Time*; and Lin basically reprises the split personality in *Chungking Express* as the faux blonde with dark glasses who takes off her wig at the end of her episode. Death is a constant, as are daydreams and nightdreams. Maggie Cheung is frail in *As Tears Go By*, is overwhelmed by lovesickness in *Days of Being Wild* and in *Ashes of Time* (she also daydreams in *Days* and dies in *Ashes*). In addition, there is amnesia, blindness and muteness. Though *Chungking Express* and *Fallen Angels* are much lighter works, evincing the comic side of the Menippean discourse, their characters are no less pathological. In fact, *Fallen Angels* is a particularly substantive model of structural and character pathology because it has even more pathological episodes and carnivalesque scenes of death (carnivalesque in the manner of parody, expressed in both a serious and funny way) than seems possible in a Wong Kar-wai movie.

We might examine these pathological episodes as they relate to each of the 'fallen angels':

- Leon Lai's killer is prone to memory loss. His apparent coolness hides not only his lack of human feelings but also his tendency or willingness to forget. This is illustrated in two episodes: the minibus episode, where he meets an old school chum (right after a killing), who actually calls him by his name 'Wong Chi-ming'[8] but whom he only vaguely recalls; and the McDonald's episode, where he meets Karen Mok's 'Blondie', an ex-girlfriend whom he has entirely forgotten. Both episodes attest to his pathological state of wilful amnesia. The original title of the song associated with the killer, 'Karmacoma' (by the group Massive Attack, rearranged by Wong's musical team of Frankie Chan and Roel Garcia), perfectly captures the character's pathology. Wong's characteristic step-printed slow motion presents the hitman walking zombie-like to his kills as if in a coma, which has arrested his karma. It is a condition that is both an occupational requirement and a hazard that seems voluntary or self-imposed. His occupation also means that he must assume a fake identity (he shows his schoolmate a photograph of a black woman and a child, who function as his 'family'), and keep an emotional distance from women. Both afflictions eventually wear him down, which he resolves by death (this being the only possible means of releasing his karma).
- Takeshi Kaneshiro's mute stopped talking at the age of five, but he 'speaks' to us through monologues. He lives and sleeps with his old father in a room in the Chungking Mansion hotel of which his father is the caretaker. We learn from his monologue that an ice-cream truck killed his mother. Our suspicion that his muteness is a strategy for avoiding interacting fully with the world can be traced to the absence of the mother, another Oedipal urge that accounts for the antisocial behaviour of Wong Kar-wai's characters (cf. the Ah Fei Yuddy's rebelliousness in *Days of Being Wild*). Wong, however, shows a benign facet of pathology in this instance: the father-and-son relationship is, on the whole, free of psychological complexes, and their episodes together stress the theme of bonding and camaraderie, touchingly conveyed in the episode of the mute's playful videoing of his father to mark his sixtieth birthday, accompanied by the Taiwanese pop number 'Thinking of You' (sung by Chyi Chin); and the episodes in which the mute breaks into shops and hawker

stalls, appropriating them to do his own businesses, are presented amusingly, with the mute's 'victims' appearing as benignly unhinged as he is. The mute, for all his antisocial instincts, at least knows the value of self-redemption ('If Buddha himself would not descend into hell, who else would?') and working hard ('There are no free lunches in this world').

• Michele Reis's middlewoman is possibly the most interesting of Wong Kar-wai's creations, and totally believable as a character. Her plausibility lies, I would suggest, in the pathology of her lovesickness. Reis may be in love with the hitman but it is not a normal kind of love. The hitman's distance determines their kind of love. She therefore loves at a distance, because in her own words, 'To know somebody well is to render him boring.' 'I'm a practical person, I know how to make myself happy,' she says, and the result is one of Wong's most self-obsessed characters, typically forsaken by love, who indulges in a freakish, fetishistic kind of love. She goes to the same pub that the hitman frequents, not to meet him but to luxuriate in the atmosphere of the place where he has been, where he has left his memory trace. There is the episode where she moves her body against the jukebox, caressing it almost as if it were a lover, recalling *Ashes of Time* where Brigitte Lin embraces a tree in a state of arousal. But here it is taken to the level of cybernetics. It is a strangely fascinating scene: the girl's dress simmers like some organic living species to the sound of Laurie Anderson's 'Speak My Language', her pouting red lips, caressing hands, ubiquitous smouldering cigarette and probing thighs exuding orgasmic sensuality, culminating with her masturbating on the hitman's bed sheet. In the lonely world of Wong Kar-wai's women, trees, horses and jukeboxes are substitutes for real lovers.

• Externally, Reis's character betrays the same languorous lack of energy as other characters in Wong's previous films. But this nonchalance, this desultory exterior, hides the desperation within. Reis gets the message that the hitman wants to terminate the partnership, but her despair is visible to the outside world only in the shakiness of her hand as she holds a cigarette. When Reis says at the end of the film, as she rides off with the mute, 'The road isn't long and I know I'll be getting off soon,' we sense that she may mean more than getting off the motorbike – her bleak mental state was evident in the earlier scene where she is eating noodles with a blank, wide-eyed stare, oblivious to the fight going on behind her. She has become completely desensitised. While the film ends at this point with the Flying Pickets' 'Only You' – a subliminal reference to her unspoken love for the hitman – it is her previous association with Laurie Anderson's 'Speak My Language' that is more suggestive of her psychological state:

Daddy, daddy ... It was just like you said
Now that the living outnumber the dead
Where I come from, it's a long thin thread
Across the ocean, down the river of red
Now that the living outnumber the dead.

- Charlie Young's woman who cries on the mute's shoulder is afflicted with the spurned lover syndrome, which results in an unstable mind (faking delight at her lover Johnny's news that he is marrying another woman, and pouring venom on 'Blondie', the woman who has supposedly captured the heart of her lover). Quite apart from the effects of this syndrome – such as her inability to forget Johnny ('When will her emotions run out of date?' the mute asks), which places her in the gallery of Wong Kar-wai characters who suffer the pain of not being able to forget – Wong highlights the theme of fakery and substitutes in the pathological episode where she and Kaneshiro search for 'Blondie' in the housing estate, and find 'her' in the shape of a discarded sex-toy dummy. They proceed to bash the dummy blonde.
- Karen Mok's 'Blondie' is a deliberate recall of Brigitte Lin's faux blonde in *Chungking Express*, but Mok is a woman seething with heat and emotion compared to Lin's ice-woman. Unlike Lin, Mok's rationale for her blonde look is not to hide her identity but rather to ensure that no one will forget her, since Lai's killer had forgotten her when she had worn her hair long. Mok has a pathological urge for people to remember her. When Lai decides to leave her, she bites his hand. 'What's the idea?' Lai asks. 'To remember me by,' she replies. 'If you don't remember my face,

you might remember my bite,' and she breaks down in tears, muttering, 'I have a face worth remembering. There's a mole on my face. Next time you pass a woman with a mole on her face, she might be me. Will you remember?'

In the world of Wong Kar-wai, love is a sickness and memory is as much an affliction as forgetfulness. But *Fallen Angels* strikes one as a catalogue of even more wide-ranging afflictions. From the episodes recounted above, the following pathological states are displayed: muteness, play-acting, self-obsession, antisocial behaviour, fake response, fake identity, violence, trespassing, mood swings and loneliness. Wong Kar-wai has reworked the theme of human alienation more comprehensively in a setting that is even more modern and futuristic than in *Chungking Express*. Here, Hong Kong is a carnivalesque cosmogony, 'a homology between the body, dream, linguistic structure and structures of desire', in Kristeva's words.[9] Hong Kong is one big metaphor.

Hong Kong is one of Italo Calvino's invisible cities, 'where no desire is lost and of which you are a part, and since it enjoys everything you do not enjoy, you can do nothing but inhabit this desire and be content'.[10] In this city, the labour of the hitman, the mute, the middlewoman and the 'Blondies', gives 'form to desire' and 'takes from desire its form'.[11] The desire is pathological, and their labour informs the pathology of the city. Like Tony Leung's apartment in *Chungking Express*, which becomes emotional and 'cries', Wong's Hong Kong, God's cursed ground on which fallen angels tread, oozes pathology. Every nook and cranny of Hong Kong sheds tears, so to speak (and it is no accident that rain is employed as a visual motif). *Fallen Angels* is Wong's most ardent Hong Kong movie. Here, Hong Kong is a fast commute between Kwun Tong (where the killer's apartment is located) and Chungking Mansion (where Reis and Kaneshiro reside), between Kowloon and Hong Kong Island (hence the emphasis on trains, minibuses, Kaneshiro's motorbike crossing the tunnel). Never before has Wong covered so much ground: gambling houses, cheap hotels, back alleyways, pubs, eateries, restaurants, street stalls, pavements, apartments, the football stadium, subway stations.

However, following on from his tendency to focus on a particular locality in his previous films (e.g. Mongkok and Lantau Island in *As Tears Go By*,
Tsimshatsui and Lan Kwai Fong in *Chungking Express*) Wong has chosen to
concentrate on Wanchai this time around. He specifically chose locations
on the older side of Wanchai, in the streets and alleys of Queen's Road East,
where, he says, the 'restaurants, the old bookshops, the grocery stores,
reflect the lifestyles of the Hong Kong people but which most probably will
disappear in the near future'. Wong claimed that he was at first not conscious of the fact that he had focused on old Wanchai, but once he became
aware of it, he sought to preserve this on film, in the same way that the old
Cantonese movies shown on late-night TV have preserved the 'disappeared
spaces' of Hong Kong.[12] Ackhar Abbas, who coined the term 'disappeared
spaces', refers to Wong Kar-wai's films as 'the most political of all', though
they have 'no overt political content', because his films 'describe mutations,
particularly of space and affectivity'.[13]

To my mind, however, *Fallen Angels* is Wong's most social and political
work, because of the messages encoded in the ambivalence of the film's
'linguistic structure' – ambivalence that arises from the 'insertion of history (society) into a text and of this text into history', as Kristeva defines
it;[14] ambivalence, therefore, embedded in the structure of the film and
manifested in the series of correlational symbolisms: mute–talk,
blonde–black, falsehood–truth, amnesia–memory, closeness–distance,
chance–determinism, death–life. Wong's moral message stems from the
intersections of the word, 'where at least one other word can be read'.[15]
Ambivalence, also, embedded in the nostalgic references to old Wanchai
and the resolutely contemporary nature of Hong Kong at large.

Ironically, Wong's Hong Kong seems more out of this world the more the
ambivalence is embedded, which is to say, the more it reminds us of Hong
Kong. Visually, his use of the distorting wide-angle lens to delineate distance as a psychological effect structures the ambivalence of the film in
terms of both its mix of genres and its description of the city. Film noir
blends with science fiction in the same sense of distance and closeness; and
Christopher Doyle's cinematography of the urban landscape achieves both a
realistic film noir look and a sci-fi ambience of Hong Kong. Like the char-

acters in previous films, the protagonists in this film come alive only at night – very late at night, it seems, for the cavernous subway stations are devoid of people, and the markets and stalls where Kaneshiro wreaks his mischief are deserted. Even McDonald's is empty. Again, the people-less landscape bespeaks the social isolation of Wong's fallen but highly mobile angels.

The halogenic lights of the passing MTR train on the elevated track of Kwun Tong shoot by like stars, the hectic lights of the late-night entertainment billboards and neon lights, close-ups of moving lights emitted by machine parts slid and slide (such as the lights from the jukebox) – all create a hallucinatory, futuristic environment that recalls Lang's *Metropolis* or Murakami's *Hardboiled Wonderland*. The swaying, slanted angles of the hand-held camerawork generate a floating effect, as if we are in a plane looking down on a world that is not quite real. The blue cross-harbour tunnel along which Kaneshiro guns his motorbike at breakneck speed resembles a stairway to outer space, and Kaneshiro, in his crash helmet, looks for all the world like an astronaut. Even the cramped rooms in which the characters live exude a quality of unrealness, like suspended space capsules. The artificiality of the environment is heightened by the interior lighting style seen in the previous films (the all blue, golds and reds), and the prominence given to objects made of artificial materials (plastic curtains, even the plastic dresses that Reis prefers). The film is yet another energising synergy of Christopher Doyle's sense of colour and William Chang's production design.

The distorting lens may be traced to the visual influence of Francis Bacon, which is particularly evident in the separate scenes of Reis and the hitman in the pub. Reis sits on the counter luxuriating in the hitman's memory trace. For a few seconds, we see a double image of her, as if through a smoked glass or distorting mirror. This strange effect is repeated later in a scene where the hitman revisits the pub and sits in the same place (he hands a coin to the bartender and instructs him to give it to Reis with the message to play song '1818' on the jukebox). It is an effect that operates on the Baconian principle seen in his paintings of deformed faces: that distortion is a means to achieve reality. Bacon had blurred and disintegrated his figures not so much to capture the effect of movement, as was the motive of the Futurists, but as a means to bring out inherent qualities, so that a portrait of a distorted face may be more real than one that merely seeks to ape a physical likeness. It is an attempt to capture the figure's memory trace, like Reis searching through the killer's garbage; and the film as a whole tries to capture Hong Kong's memory traces.

Cinematically, the post-modern noir approach contains traces yet again of Haruki Murakami, but more particularly it smacks of Seijun Suzuki, whose *Branded to Kill* (1967) carries the blueprint of the relationship between Leon Lai's hitman and Michele Reis's middlewoman. Suzuki's film centres on a 'Number Three Hitman' named Hanada (played by Jo Shishido) and a *femme fatale* named Misako (played by Annu Mari), who hires his services as a killer. Hanada is immediately attracted to Misako, but she hates men and harbours the hope of dying, though for the moment she declares, 'I am already a corpse.' Misako has set up Hanada, but she fills him with such erotic desire that he cannot bring himself to kill her. This marks his downfall as a professional killer ('I'm a failure as a hitman,' he says, 'because I couldn't kill someone I had to kill'). Wong's variation of this relationship reverses the suffering complex: it is Reis who is brought down by the sexual charge that she feels for the hitman (whom she may have set up for the final kill); and the hitman is the walking corpse with a hint of misogyny. Suzuki's *femme fatale* is associated with dead birds and butterflies, and feels nothing when Hanada tries to make love to her. Reis is associated with plastic dresses, a woman self-wrapped in cellophane making vicarious love with the memory traces of the hitman. Suzuki's Tokyo and Wong's Hong Kong share the same sense of noir desperation and futuristic distance.

In the end, however, the references are to Wong's own films. The despair of the female characters is all of a piece with the women in the preceding film, *Ashes of Time*, and in *Days of Being Wild*. Michele Reis's middlewoman recalls Leslie Cheung's Ouyang Feng; Leon Lai's nihilism reminds us of Yuddy's; while Takeshi Kaneshiro's infectious whimsy is in line with the deep emotionalism of Jacky Cheung's performances in *As Tears Go By*, *Days of Being Wild* and *Ashes of Time*. Then again, Takeshi's presence reminds us that no matter that 'There is a difference', *Fallen Angels* will forever be linked with *Chungking Express*. Kaneshiro becomes mute after eating a can of pineapples with an expired use-by date; his father works as a caretaker inside Chungking Mansion; he himself ends up in the Midnight Express, while Charlie Young waits for her new lover in an airhostess's uniform. Kaneshiro also reinvokes the maxim of people brushing by each other and sparking off karma. Reis spends time cleaning up the hitman's apartment in his absence, exactly like Faye Wong does with Tony Leung's flat. Then, there is the ubiquitous big clock, seen in the hitman's apartment. It is as if Wong Kar-wai has left signposts for us, imprinting a history of his film-making on this film. Or is he merely poking fun at us: the pathology of the film-maker?

Seven

Wong's Buenos Aires Affair:
Happy Together (1997)

An Affair to Remember

To many, *Happy Together* marks a new milestone in the career of Wong Kar-wai, insofar as it is a film about exile, a theme that seems to have emerged willy-nilly in Wong's cinema for the first time (if we discount Yuddy's adventures in the Philippines in *Days of Being Wild* or Ouyang Feng's retreat into the western desert in *Ashes of Time* where exile is not the main theme). Because *Happy Together* is set in Argentina, a country as far away from Hong Kong as any country could be, the sense of exile is all the more palpable, and it is the first Wong Kar-wai film entirely set in a foreign country. 'In a place which is completely strange, one can start all over again,' Wong says,[1] echoing that very same refrain that characterises the Leslie Cheung–Tony Leung Chiu-wai relationship in the movie.

Cheung and Leung play two gay men who go to Argentina to resuscitate an affair, then fall out, separate and meet again. The movie focuses on Leung as Lai Yiu-fai, who harbours a guilty conscience over the money he stole to go to Argentina, and which has estranged him from his father. This makes him more sober and level-headed than Cheung (as Ho Po-wing), who is carefree and promiscuous. Having spent all his money travelling with Ho, Lai has to find work in a tango bar after their separation to earn enough to return to Hong Kong. Ho, meanwhile, is working as a gay escort, 'dancing and tricking his night away without reflection or remorse'.[2] After meeting Ho by chance, a reunion takes place, at first haphazardly, but later more prolongedly when Ho turns up at Lai's apartment, his hands crushed by a trick for stealing a watch, and Lai virtually nurses him back to health. As they start over again, Lai hides Ho's passport, perhaps hoping that he would

'Let's start all over again': Leslie Cheung and Tony Leung in *Happy Together*

remain with him in a more stable relationship. This backfires; Ho leaves, and Lai spends the rest of his time working at various jobs, including a stint as a cook in a Chinese restaurant, where he befriends a young Taiwanese, played by Chang Chen. Lai eventually returns to Hong Kong, by way of a stopover in Taipei, as Ho sinks into emotional depression.

According to Wong, Lai and Ho's sojourn in Argentina is a means to 'escape reality'.[3] Like his characters, Wong reveals, he was sick of the constant questions about 1 July 1997 (the date of Hong Kong's handover to China): 'Hence we wanted to escape but the more we wanted to escape the more we became inseparable from Hong Kong. No matter where we went, Hong Kong was always with us.'[4] The theme of exile is therefore connected to the 1997 deadline that was casting a shadow over many Hong Kong lives, particularly those of gay men. In making his two main characters gay and cutting them adrift in a faraway country, Wong was making a point about the socio-political ramifications of 1997: the fact that the one group in Hong Kong that felt the most anxious and had the most to lose in terms of indi-

vidual and civil liberties was the gay community. Wong had convinced Leslie
Cheung, long identified as gay, to appear in *Happy Together* because 'Hong
Kong needed to make a real gay film before 1997'.[5]

Thus, in addition to the theme of exile, the perception of *Happy Together*
as a milestone can also be felt in Wong's attempt to make a 'real gay film' and
to concretise the 1997 issue by depicting two Hong Kong men consciously
escaping from the contemporary time-reality of Hong Kong by depositing
themselves in another time, another place. The further away that Wong
travels, the more 1997 and Hong Kong become visible issues, just as in Italo
Calvino's *Invisible Cities*, where Marco Polo's descriptions of imaginary
cities told to Kublai Khan are really descriptions of Venice.

But while Hong Kong and 1997 are the real issues, the movie's space is
Buenos Aires (Hong Kong is seen only upside down in a few shots towards
the end of the film), where time is somewhat lost, since the seasons are
reversed, and past and present time are muddled by intercalating black-
and-white memory episodes into the colour scheme of present time. The
film takes place over a period from May 1995, when the protagonists first
arrive in Argentina, to February 1997, the time when Lai Yiu-fai wakes up in
a Taipei hotel on the day that Deng Xiaoping's death is announced on TV.

Though Wong has denied that he had intended Lai and Ho as 'signifiers'
of the China–Hong Kong relationship, he has said that the use of the title
'Happy Together' (and one might add, the song at the end of the film) was
meant to denote the hope that 'we could all be happy together after 1997, but
no one can give a decisive answer as to what will really happen after July 1,
1997'.[6] In as much as Wong has ever made a political movie – and *Happy
Together*, in my opinion, qualifies as his most political movie to date – it is
conditioned by the 1997 deadline, highlighting its spiritually debilitating
effects on two Hong Kong men; and Wong attempting to make a gay movie
before 1 July, 1997 catches up with it (the movie was released in Hong Kong
at the end of April 1997).

The movie is really a protest about time, but in its state of exile, time is
reset. 'We all have our own calendars', Wong has been quoted as saying on
many occasions, and it is perhaps fair to say that the calendars of the protagonists in *Happy Together* are tuned to the state of exile, the outcome of

which is inevitably tragic, though not without satirical undertones. *Happy Together* may also be seen as a product of Wong's own feeling of exile, a state of existence brought about by his outsider status as a Shanghainese in Cantonese Hong Kong and his reputation as the perennial *enfant terrible* of the Hong Kong film industry.

It is interesting that Buenos Aires was the city that realised Wong's own sense of exile, which arguably remained immanent in him as a cinematic theme almost from the start of his career: for example, Andy Lau's retreat into Lantau Island in *As Tears Go By* may be the first sign of this theme. In poetic language, Wong described Buenos Aires as 'a land of zero degree, with neither east nor west, has neither day nor night, which is neither cold nor warm'. In this land, Wong concluded, he 'learned the feeling of exile'.[7] The choice of Buenos Aires came about because Wong had originally wanted to make a movie adapted from Manuel Puig's novel *The Buenos Aires Affair*. Wong abandoned this plan as the production proceeded, although during shooting, the movie continued to be known by the novel's title.[8]

We do not know why Wong gave up the idea of adapting Puig's novel, but the book itself might suggest some answers. It deals with the sexual psychology of two tormented individuals: Gladys, an artist possessed by feelings of sexual inadequacy from youth who wears dark glasses to hide the fact that she has only one eye (having lost the other as a result of a blow to the head when she was raped as a student in New York); and Leo, an art critic with a troubled history as a child and young adult due to his oversized penis, which many years earlier had led him to kill a young hustler who had propositioned him, a murder that has remained undetected and that now haunts him, affecting his sexual life (impotent in normal relationships, he finds fulfilment only with prostitutes).

The novel reaches surreal Hitchcockian dimensions in describing the love affair between Leo and Gladys, who both suffer in their own ways from a complex of guilt and sexual anxiety, which Leo tries to resolve by conceiving a bizarre plan to murder Gladys. Both characters are finally bound together in a strange, kinky fusion. Both are chronic masturbators (in hindsight, Gladys is probably the original model for the Michelle Reis character in *Fallen Angels*), and Leo also attempts to exorcise his fears through psychotherapy.

The sexual pathology of these two characters is slightly beyond the realm of Wong Kar-wai. Whatever may be said about Wong, his artistic personality is essentially characterised by a certain conservatism in sexual matters, being more attuned to delineating the cerebral rather than the physical depths of human relationships. In Wong's hands, *The Buenos Aires Affair* eventually transmuted into a story of two Hong Kong individuals based on the novel's broad theme of an impossible love affair between two human beings brought together by shared defects of character that might be attributed to prescribed sexual norms in society (the notion that certain sexual behaviour is abnormal).[9]

The novel is suffused with descriptions of graphic sex, which at times makes it almost pornographic. Even Wong could not entirely get over the sexual energy generated by the novel, and perhaps as a tribute to it, launches straight into a lovemaking scene as the film opens, and it remains the most graphic sex scene in all of his movies so far. However, the scene is a one-off; his lovers are not shown making love again in the course of the movie (or at least not in as sustained a manner). The scene is a device to step over the novel's focus on sexual pathology and to refocus the story on Wong's own narrative orientation of how two people communicate or miscommunicate.[10]

Happy Together also recalls another Puig novel, *Kiss of the Spider Woman*, which may in fact be a more fitting model in its depiction of a relationship between two men in enclosed circumstances along the theme that love is free of gender: Wong's contention being that homosexual love is no different from heterosexual love.[11] I will return to the connection with *Kiss of the Spider Woman* later, but as far as *The Buenos Aires Affair* is concerned, the movie subsequently has little association with its supposed source. As in *Ashes of Time*, where Wong made a film that had little or no connection with its apparent source novel (Jin Yong's *The Eagle Shooting Heroes*), Wong probably proceeded with his project on the whim of adapting *The Buenos Aires Affair* but with the ultimate aim of using the novel as a jumping-off stage for his own evolutionary method of adapting a story by an established author. The method 'evolves' another story out of the supposed source during the filming process itself, depending not on a completed screenplay but on the circumstances and improvisation of following an outline, unsure how the film will turn out until the very end. It is the *association* with the novel that seems more important than the actual plot of the source material.

In this regard, another Argentinian connection should be mentioned. For the Chinese title, Wong had wanted to use 'Chunguang Zhaxie' (which translates roughly as 'Outburst of Spring Light'). He discovered that it was the title given to Antonioni's *Blow-Up* (1966) when it was released in Hong Kong, and that *Blow-Up* was adapted from a short story by the Argentinian writer Julio Cortázar. Struck by the coincidence, he decided to use the Chinese title: 'I feel that everything is connected by fate, and film is also like that.'[12]

As fate would have it, *Happy Together* shares a closer affinity with Cortázar's *Hopscotch* than with *The Buenos Aires Affair*. *Hopscotch* is a novel about an Argentinian writer in Paris, Horacio Oliveira, whose relationship with a mistress, La Maga, a kindred Latin American, is beset with problems of an inner spiritual kind. When La Maga disappears after the death of her child, Oliveira, who feels the guilt of this disappearance (compounded too by his sense of complicity over the child's death, which he first discovers but withholds from La Maga in one of the novel's most memorable chapters), returns to Buenos Aires after endless soul-searching on the streets of Paris and an unnerving encounter with a *clocharde* on the bank of the Seine that leads to their arrest for indecency. The spiritual crisis in Oliveira's existence is magnified by living in Paris, where he remains tied to his country in a ritual of keeping himself up to date in a 'correspondence with Latin America', but the more he keeps himself up to date, the more he feels the anguish and complication of exile:

> To bring up to date: what an expression. To do. To do something, to do good, to make water, to make time, action in all of its possibilities. But behind all action there was a protest, because all doing meant leaving *from* in order to arrive *at*, or moving something so that it would be here and not there, or going into a house instead of not going in or instead of going into the one next door; in other words, every act entailed the admission of a lack, of something not yet done and which could have been done, the tacit protest in the face of continuous evidence of a lack, of a reduction, of the inadequacy of the present moment.[13]

Oliveira's relationship with La Maga proceeds in a fashion of love and acrimony in about equal measures, 'for we loved each other in a sort of dialectic of magnet and iron filings, attack and defense, handball and wall'.[14] The impossibility of harmony is seemingly determined by, on La Maga's side, 'a sort of monotonous and persistent speech, an insistent Berlitz, I-love-you, I-love-you', and, on Oliveira's side, by 'an obedience to desire' that obfuscates love. 'And time? Everything begins again, there is no absolute.'[15] The wheel turns in the same fashion over and over again; the lovers make love, quarrel, call a truce and there is a precarious happiness, in the midst of which, as Oliveira intones in a monologue, 'I held out my hand and touch the tangled ball of yarn which is Paris, its infinite material all wrapped up around itself, the precipitate of its atmosphere falling on its windows and forming images of clouds and garrets.'[16]

Paris, in this instance, is a substitute for Buenos Aires, just as Buenos Aires is a substitute for Hong Kong. Like Buenos Aires for Lai Yiu-fai and Ho Po-wing, Paris for Oliveira and La Maga is a city to make love in, but it represents a lack, an emptiness and a lost opportunity to find happiness: 'Too late, always too late, because even though we made love so many times, happiness must have been something else, something sadder perhaps than this peace, this pleasure, a mood of unicorn or island, an endless fall in immobility.'[17]

The characters of *Happy Together* do not fall into immobility; on the contrary, they are endlessly mobile, which shows that happiness is forever eluding them. Right after the opening lovemaking scene – when the film proceeds in black and white, denoting the flashback time from the perspective of Lai Yiu-fai[18] – we see Lai and Ho Po-wing on the road as would-be tourists driving a used car towards the Argentina–Brazil border to visit the Iguazú Falls. This was to be the climactic moment of their affair in Argentina; after visiting the Falls, they would then return to Hong Kong. However, they lose their way and immediately begin to bicker. The lovers decide to separate, Ho declaring that he has grown bored with Lai and that maybe if they were to meet again, they could 'start all over again'.

We see them standing by the side of the lonely highway trying to hitch a ride after abandoning their car. They never get to the Falls together (in the end, Lai goes there alone), but Wong affords us a spectacular view of the tourist attraction (in colour, denoting a flash-forward but essentially the real time of his narrative). As Chris Doyle shoots it (an overhead shot of the waterfall, accompanied on the soundtrack by the voice of Brazilian singer Caetano Veloso and his rendition of the sensual 'Cucurucucu Paloma'), it looks like no other waterfall. The texture of the descending water and the vapours rising upwards create an unreal, dreamlike sensation. Ho and Lai do not get to see it as planned, and thus it becomes a symbol of lost hope – the too-late-ness of finding happiness together – remaining in the mind's eye long after the film has ended (in this sense, the Falls symbolise the eternal flash-forward, the future, as well as happiness in real time: 'the endless fall in immobility').

A Man and a (Wo)man

The conceit in Cortázar's novel is that love in a foreign country leads to nothingness and that happiness is elusive, while in Puig, sexual identity and behaviour determine one's character. As the movie's English title emphasises happiness, and Lai and Ho are only occasionally happy together and more often contemplating starting over, the concept of happiness is a primary theme and one that connects it more strongly to Cortázar than Puig. Wong's theme of love, or more specifically genderless love, is secondary, though quite tendentious from his perspective, while homosexual identity as a theme appears to be irrelevant if not entirely non-existent. In fact, some homosexual critics hotly dispute the contention that *Happy Together* is first, a gay movie, and second, is about love not related to gender. Such is the view of Edward Lam, a Hong Kong critic, writer and theatre director also well known as an advocate of homosexual rights. In a review of the movie published in *City Entertainment*, Lam writes that *Happy Together* is not a gay movie, 'because it is wholly guided by heterosexual ideology', disagreeing with the claim that the movie is about 'love' unrelated to sexual orientation.[19] Lam finds fault with the casting of Tony Leung and Leslie Cheung as the lovers, arguing that Wong was essentially typecasting, so that the audience would identify Cheung as the typical gay (feminine, coyly bashful, unconventional, promiscuous and conceited) and Leung as a straight man playing a gay man. Tony Leung, Lam writes, is a victim of the 'gay' Leslie Cheung – he waits after him, looks after him, and is tolerant and loyal. His every behaviour represents 'love' in the heterosexual norms familiar to a mass audience. Therefore, he is noble and worthy of sympathy. Add in his masculine looks and his choice of being the dominant partner during lovemaking, he represents the typical 'husband' in the hetero-sexual love relationship. As a result, Leslie Cheung, being the unfaithful partner, deserves all the anguish he gets as he weeps uncontrollably into his blanket. When Cheung is cooped up suffering his emotional torment, Leung goes to the waterfall. He is like all real 'men', possessing liberty and mobility, and even becomes the object of Zhang Zhen's admiration. *Happy Together* tells its audience that we cannot but choose the 'male' side of homosexuality, or at the very least, that we should choose the 'normal' male as a model, which is Tony Leung.[20]

Lam's critique highlights the idea that there are male and female models in Wong's film, and that Leslie Cheung is typecast as the 'female' partner to build upon public perceptions of the actor – the public being familiar with Cheung's gay persona largely through his role as the female impersonator in Chen Kaige's *Farewell My Concubine* (1993).

I would suggest that the 'typecasting' of Cheung and Leung in respective 'female' and 'male' roles is a perception heightened by the total lack of female protagonists in the film: *Happy Together* being the first Wong Kar-wai film in which there are no women in major or minor roles. We know from *Buenos Aires Zero Degree*, the 1999 documentary about the making of *Happy Together* (which includes out-takes and deleted scenes from the film), that Wong did feature two female characters (one played by the singer Shirley Kwan in her very first film appearance) but decided to cut them out entirely. The movie as it stands features three men, the third man being Chang Chen (Zhang Zhen in Pinyin) as the Taiwanese kitchen hand whom Lai Yiu-fai befriends and who, in a telling scene, rebuffs a girl, a fellow worker, as she asks him for a date. 'I don't like her voice,' Chang says, adding an untypical touch of misogyny into the cinema of Wong Kar-wai. Because of the lack of women, Wong almost forces us to search for female surrogates in his male characters. There is a very brief shot in *Buenos Aires Zero Degree* of Leslie

Typecast in male and female roles? Tony Leung and Leslie Cheung in *Happy Together*

Cheung in drag – a fascinating and curious piece of evidence from Wong's creative process that reveals what he might have intended in drawing out the characterisation of Ho Po-wing, and also provides a clue to the conceptualising of Cheung in the 'female' role.[21]

Here we come to Puig's *Kiss of the Spider Woman* as the chief inspiration behind the idea of the female role in the drama between Ho Po-wing and Lai Yiu-fai. Towards the end of the novel, Valentin, a political prisoner with straight male macho tendencies, undergoes a conversion through his relationship with his cellmate, Molina (in jail for corruption of minors), who adopts the position of the surrogate woman. Molina does not understand the concept of equality between the 'man of the house and the woman of the house' when Valentin tries to explain that otherwise 'their relation becomes a form of exploitation'. But Molina gets his kick out of the fact that 'when a man embraces you ... you may feel a little bit frightened', to which Valentin responds, 'No, that's all wrong ... To be a woman, you don't have to be ... a martyr. ... This business of being a man, it doesn't give any special rights to anyone.'[22] Valentin is asking Molina to make a political commitment 'to act like a man' and not to act as a surrogate woman.

When Molina eventually gets out of prison, Valentin makes him promise 'that you're going to make them respect you, that you're not going to allow anyone to treat you badly, or exploit you. Because no one has the right to exploit anyone.'[23] The revolutionary Valentin becomes Puig's mouthpiece of homosexual rights. In Edward Lam's critique, Leslie Cheung is 'typecast' as a gay man acting as a surrogate woman to Tony Leung's 'male' persona, which seems like a retrogression into the mindset of old wives' tales (according to Valentin, Molina has been fed 'an old wives' tale by whoever filled your head with that nonsense').

Yet, Lam may have missed the point that Wong is trying to make. In his own way, Wong is trying to demonstrate that the business of being a man does not give anyone special rights. In fact, he parodies the notion of the surrogate woman and the idea of acting like a man in the scenes where Lai looks after Ho in his apartment after the latter has been beaten up. These scenes constitute the heart of the film, and contain some very funny and touching moments between the two men. In one of the funny scenes, Ho, his hands bandaged and recuperating from his injuries, is lying on the bed as Lai sleeps on the sofa. He goes over to the sofa and snuggles up to Lai.

LAI: Why do you want to sleep here where we're so pressed for space?

HO: Because I like it.

LAI: Don't you think this is too small for us?

HO: No it's comfy.

(Ho gives Lai a bite)

LAI: Ow! Why are you biting me?

HO: I'm hungry.

LAI: Do you want to sleep here on the sofa?

HO: Why?

LAI: Because I'll sleep on the bed then.

HO: Don't go on about it. Just go to sleep.

LAI: Or else you take the bed and I'll sleep on the sofa.

HO: What an old fusspot you are.

(Lai stands up and gets into the bed. Ho follows, and again tries to snuggle up to
   Lai)

HO: You are not so heartless, are you?

LAI: We are tight for space.

HO: Not at all.

(Ho climbs on top of Lai)

HO: I'll get on top and we'll just sleep like this.

(Ho lies on top, his face digging into Lai's neck)

Lai: So you want to sleep here?

Ho: Are you going to be like that?

(Lai pushes him aside and tries to get up)

Ho: All right … I'll sleep here. Let's sleep together.

Lai: All right. Go to sleep. But don't you trifle with me.

Ho: Who, me? Don't you trifle with me.

(He quickly plants his lips on Lai's cheek)

Give us a kiss! Good night.

If we accept Lam's notion of the typecast male and female roles played by
Leung and Cheung, the scene above works as a parody of male and female
roles: Ho getting on top of Lai and Lai feeling a little bit frightened ('Don't
you trifle with me'). The whole business in these scenes (including the one
I have cited and others which show Leung nursing Cheung, being forced to
cook when he has a fever, cleaning the apartment, etc.) inverts Leung's male
role and makes him the 'female'. Lam interprets this as Leung falling victim
to Cheung, but Wong's sense of parody is quite plain – and the parody gains
its substance from the connection with *Kiss of the Spider Woman*, where
Molina is a living parody of a homosexual and it is Valentin who pleads for
homosexual rights. As a post-modern film, *Happy Together* assumes that the
notion of male and female roles in homosexual relationships has passed its
time. Sexual relations are free of gender, as Wong stresses, and time moves
on, which renders the notion of gender in Lai and Ho's relationship mean-
ingless and therefore worthy of parody.

Happy Together is marked by its premonition of 1997 as the end of time,
a notion that in hindsight is quite absurd but which unbalances the well-

being and happiness of Hong Kong people. In a sense, Wong's film evinces the kind of 'inverted millenarianism' that Fredric Jameson refers to in his seminal essay on post-modernism,[24] manifesting the end of time as a personal crisis in the Buenos Aires affair of Ho and Lai.

In order to look at the nature of Ho and Lai's crisis, I come back to the image of the Iguazú Falls that we see in colour at the beginning. The Falls are essentially the carrier of real time in the film, as they intrude into the monochromatic memory scenes of Lai and Ho lost on their way to visit the tourist attraction. To Wong, the Falls represent sexual energy[25] (and the way that he presents them as a force of nature, sexual energy is really a notion unto itself, isolated from gender or even species). I have suggested that the Falls are a symbol of happiness, which is elusive on account of their flow in real time: it is lost if it is not grasped. It is difficult to keep track of: 'happy, *ergo* futureless', to quote Cortázar in *Hopscotch*. But the characters are not happy and they seem trapped in the end of time, without future. Seen today, the power of the film resides in its sense of being a memorial to the pre-1997 anxiety of Hong Kong, and by some stroke of fate, the film today also acts as a memorial for Leslie Cheung, who is seen sprawled in despair on a street pavement towards the end of the film, almost as if he had fallen down from a great height (in real life, Cheung jumped to his death). It was Wong, after all, who was best able to capture Cheung's real-life despair that led to his suicide.

The Falls are present as a symbol throughout the film in the shape of the night-lamp that reflects their image when it shines. The night-lamp represents not only a hope but also an illusion. In many ways, the movie is shot in a style that makes it illusionary, an end of time. Doyle's cinematography reflects the subjectivity of his characters and their psychic energy. Colour is the principal means of expression: the chroma is heightened; gold turns into an aggressive orange and red; there is bright yellow; the blue is hallucinatory like the light we see on recovering from an anaesthetic after an operation. Doyle uses colour in a Fauvist manner, basing it on feeling, choosing colour to fit sensation rather than reality. The use of the colour red as a theme (particularly striking in the abattoir scene where Lai washes the blood of slaughtered cattle from the pavement, and in the kitchen scene where Lai puts a pot containing a red liquid on the table) makes more sense in the light of Wong's original plan to have Lai commit suicide (as documented in *Buenos Aires Zero Degree*, which shows a deleted scene of blood flowing from Lai's cut wrists), but red nevertheless works as a representation of the anger and frustration that characterises Lai's relationship with Ho.

Doyle even manages to evoke emotion in the monochromatic scenes, as in the shot of Ho taking Lai's hand, which is holding a cigarette, to light his own (in the scene where Lai returns the watch to Ho), during which he gradually overexposes the shot to intensify the white, creating a sensation that the actors are being consumed by heat as they suck on their cigarettes. The scene literally sizzles with suppressed feeling. Another memorable episode is the one of Lai and Ho dancing the tango in the kitchen to the music of Astor Piazzolla. The scene is lit by a skylight; absorbed in each other and in their dance, the lovers appear like performers on stage under the spotlight. William Chang's art direction emphasises interesting geometric patterns in those monochromatic scenes that take place at the Bar Sur when Lai re-encounters Ho after their separation. Ho is wearing a checked jacket that complements the bar's floor tiles, as well as the cobblestones and brickwork on the pavement outside, where Lai paces about trying to see what Ho is doing inside. Ho's checked jacket becomes prominent as he gets into a taxi and turns around to watch Lai as the taxi drives away to the electric guitar strains of Frank Zappa's 'Chunga's Revenge'.

The setting of Lai's apartment is fittingly baroque, as evocative as Van Gogh's *Night Café* interior and less soothing than Matisse's richly patterned backgrounds. The walls of Lai's room are covered with decoratively gaudy and mismatched wallpaper offcuts and equally mismatched ceramic tiles, and a vivid blue lamp hangs overhead, while the Iguazú Falls night-lamp flickers luminously and mysteriously on the bedside table. The result is a pulsating, restless, baroque atmosphere, in which the lovers clash, fight and wrestle for emotional control.

Like artists who willingly incorporate 'accidents' into their art, Doyle and Chang use ink blotches, smears and stains on mirrors and other props as evidence of spontaneity and as testaments to the process of making art. Doyle shoots against the sun, which refracts on the camera lens creating bubbles of light in the scenes of the kitchen hands playing football and in the strange but wonderful effect of Tony Leung's face resting on a huge light bubble; the water of the Iguazú Falls condenses on the camera lens during Lai's visit, creating a sensation of being immersed in water. Doyle's photography has the spontaneity of the brush strokes and gestural techniques of a de Kooning or Jackson Pollock. It enhances the experimental and improvisatory style of Wong Kar-wai's film-making, never for a moment degenerating into self-indulgence or loss of craftsmanship, but remaining completely at the service of the director.

Happy Together is a work in which Doyle invested as much, if not more, of his time and talent as Wong. As a result, it is possibly the best looking of Wong's films. In *Buenos Aires Zero Degree*, we learn that Doyle stayed behind to shoot more cover scenes after Wong left Argentina, a sign of the cameraman's dedication and professionalism; but Wong's absence was the absence of the author in the land of exile. It was time for him to confront once more the reality of Hong Kong and 1997, to 'start all over again'.

Wong did not have a definite ending for the film in mind and had at first thought of leaving Lai in Argentina at its conclusion, but then decided, based on his own and his crew's subjective longing for home as the shooting dragged on longer than expected, that it would be more fitting after all to have Lai return to Hong Kong. He was thus relying on the personal feelings of the film's makers to finish the story rather than any logical method of developing the storyline and finding an appropriate ending. As it turns out, Leslie Cheung is left behind in the armpits of Buenos Aires in deep despair; Chang wanders to the end of the world; and Tony Leung returns to Hong Kong.

The film ends with the scene of Leung, during a stopover in Taipei, sitting inside a train on Taipei's metro system, accompanied by Danny Chung's rendition of 'Happy Together'. There is a subjective shot of the train moving on the elevated track and stopping at a station. It is as if time, in the shape of the moving train, has caught up with Lai Yiu-fai and hence with Hong Kong. 'Happy Together is a full stop, the end of a certain period of life,' Wong says in *Buenos Aires Zero Degree*. At the time, his statement might not have seemed quite as poignant as it does now. Since *Happy Together*,

Wong has gone back to the past (*In the Mood for Love*) and forward to the future (*2046*). It does appear that after 1 July 1997, time has ended. Yet the image of the Iguazú Falls persists, endlessly churning. Depending on how we see it – whether as the actual image or the reflection on the lamp – time is either real or an illusion.

Eight

Betrayed by Maggie Cheung: *In the Mood for Love* (2000)

The Beginning of the Affair

Of all Wong's projects, *In the Mood for Love* has one of the more complicated and fascinating evolutions. By piecing together various accounts of what Wong had said in interviews, his next film after *Happy Together* was a story called *Summer in Beijing*. Wong referred to this project as early as April 1997, during an interview to publicise *Happy Together* published in *City Entertainment*, in which he said he had planned to finish *Summer in Beijing* before the 1 July¹ deadline for Hong Kong's handover to China. This suggests, first, that he was already in the middle of shooting the film (perhaps even as he was working on *Happy Together*), and second, that he had conceived the project as another pre-97 work along the lines of *Happy Together*. However, Wong hinted that he was unlikely to finish the project by 1 July, and that it would therefore signify 'a new beginning' in his works, one that would touch on the Hong Kong–China relationship post-97.²

To this end, Wong began scouting locations in Beijing itself. At some point during this process, the project transmuted into a futuristic story about Beijing and was given a new title, *2046*, but retained a definite connection to the 1997 issue (*2046* marking the end of the fifty-year period during which Hong Kong's economic and political system, as China had promised, would remain unchanged). *Summer in Beijing* (with its original pre-97 framework) was now an abandoned project, but *2046* still appeared tentative, because Wong could not get permission to film in Beijing. He then took the project to Macao, but by this time (around mid-1998), it had further evolved into three stories under the title 'A Story about Food', involving an affair between Tony Leung and Maggie Cheung set in a world of restaurants and noodle shops.[3] The project eventually ended up being shot in Bangkok, and while Wong was working on the story that became *In the Mood for Love*,[4] originally intended as one-third of a movie, he decided to discard the other two episodes. Thus, *In the Mood for Love* became a separate project that evolved out of several other projects: 'Summer in Beijing', 'A Story about Food' and '2046'.

2046 survived as an ongoing project, one that he had committed himself to making during the shooting of *In the Mood for Love*. In the fifteen months that it took Wong to make the latter film, he was also shooting scenes for 2046 back to back. In what has now become his own inimitable style of making movies, Wong decided to merge the two films, 'so maybe in future when you see 2046 you will see something of *In the Mood for Love*, and when you see *In the Mood for Love* there will be something of 2046'.[5]

Since the release in 2000 of *In the Mood for Love*, 2046 has consumed Wong like an obsession, compelling him to shoot in Beijing, Shanghai, Hong Kong and Macao on top of the original footage that he shot in Bangkok during the making of *In the Mood for Love*. As a result of these extraordinary circumstances of evolution and production, *In the Mood for Love* inevitably suffers from its nature as an extended segment rather than a story originally conceived in its own right, an argument to which I will return later. However, these circumstances are fully in keeping with Wong's impromptu method of film-making inspired by the fragmentary scrapbook structures of the novels of Puig and Cortázar. This method consolidates Wong's tendency to conceive and write his stories according to the short-story format, which determines an elliptical and minimalist narrative style that distinguishes all of the director's films to date (Wong's films are best seen as a series of interconnecting short stories even within a single film, with chapter headings divided by characters rather than whole, single and separate stories).

In the Mood for Love returns to the atmosphere of Hong Kong in the 1960s that Wong described so well in *Days of Being Wild*. Hence, there is a temptation to view the film as the unofficial second part of *Days of Being Wild*. The connection with Wong's second movie is also emphasised by Maggie Cheung's appearance. Cheung plays a married woman with the maiden

Mutual suspicions mark the beginning of a love affair (*In the Mood for Love*)

name of So Lai-chen, the same name as her character in *Days of Being Wild*. Did Wong intend the two characters to be one and the same? If so, then Lai-chen has obviously evolved from being the lovesick, single young woman of the first film into a more mature, if still emotionally vulnerable, married woman in the later film. Given that ten years divide the two works, Cheung's appearance – though ageless – has a poise and sophistication that matches her new role. In terms of the chronology of the two films, two years separate the events: *Days of Being Wild* begins in 1960, while *In the Mood for Love* starts in 1962; and it may be said that the transition of So Lai-chen from young fledgling to graceful swan does appear somewhat implausible. Despite the correlation between the two films, it is probably best to see them as separate works. The differences of theme and subject matter set the two films apart: one deals with the wildness and insecurity of unmarried youth, the other with settled adults approaching middle age.

The story of *In the Mood for Love* rotates around marriage and the premise (or perhaps the illusion) of fidelity – a theme that in fact makes the film closer to *Ashes of Time*, where Wong depicts the psychological effects that

various real, pseudo and de facto marriage relationships have wrought on
his characters. There is also a connection with *Happy Together* in that both
films share the central theme of lovers coming together and breaking apart.
So Lai-chen and Chow Mo-wan (Tony Leung Chiu-wai) are neighbouring
tenants in rooming apartments. They each suspect that their respective
spouses are having an affair, as they have both gone on a long trip to Japan.
Their suspicions are confirmed when Chow invites Lai-chen to tea:

CHOW: I have asked you out because I wanted to find out something from you.
    It's about your handbag. Where can one buy a handbag like that?
LAI-CHEN: Why do you ask?
CHOW: I want to buy one just like it as a birthday gift for my wife.
LAI-CHEN: You'd have to ask my husband. He bought it on one of his trips
    abroad. He said you can't buy it in Hong Kong.
CHOW: Oh, then forget it.
LAI-CHEN: There's something I want to ask you too.
CHOW: What?
LAI-CHEN: Where did you buy your tie?
CHOW: I wouldn't know. My wife bought it when she went abroad. She said you
    can't buy it in Hong Kong.
LAI-CHEN: What a coincidence. My husband has one just like it. He said it was a
    gift from his boss.
CHOW: My wife has a handbag just like yours.
LAI-CHEN: I know. I saw it…What do you want to say?
(Chow does not answer)
LAI-CHEN: I thought I was the only one who knew.

Thus begins Chow Mo-wan's and Lai-chen's own affair, but it is a liaison
handled with typical Chinese reserve and repressed desire. As a romantic
film with a moral-ethical dimension, it recalls a long line of distinguished
films: Lean's *Brief Encounter* (1945), Fei Mu's *Spring in a Small City* (1948),
Douglas Sirk's *All That Heaven Allows* (1955) and *Imitation of Life* (1959), or
the film versions of Graham Greene's *The End of the Affair*. There are also
echoes of the melodramas of Japanese director Mikio Naruse: *Repast* (1951),

Floating Clouds (1955), and *When a Woman Ascends the Stairs* (1960). Wong himself was particularly struck by the early sing-song melodramas of the Hong Kong cinema featuring the singer-actress Zhou Xuan, *An All-Consuming Love* (1947) and *Song of a Songstress* (1948): the Chinese title of *In the Mood for Love* is in fact the title of a song, 'Huayang de Nianhua', sung by Zhou Xuan in *An All-Consuming Love* which is also heard in Wong's film. However, the one film that it most resembles in terms of plot and style is *Spring in a Small City* (remade by Tian Zhuangzhuang, who entitled his version *Springtime in a Small Town*, released in 2002). *Spring in a Small City* is the seminal work that sets the aesthetic and moral standard for the kind of romance melodrama that *In the Mood for Love* evokes: the friend of a woman's sick husband visits; he turns out to be the wife's ex-lover; old feelings are rekindled, but the man and woman pull back from the affair; the husband realises what is going on and attempts suicide; he survives and reclaims the affections of his wife; the friend leaves; his affair with the woman is temporary and impressionistic, never fully consummated, like Chow's affair with So Lai-chen.

Wong has barely mentioned *Spring in a Small City* in his interviews. To foreign journalists, he cited the influence of Hitchcock's *Vertigo* (1958), describing *In the Mood for Love* as being 'all about suspense', while also claiming that he was influenced by Bresson and Antonioni.[6] The Hitchcock reference is of more significance, being discernible in the way that Wong presents the affair between Chow Mo-wan and So Lai-chen, building up their liaison on a note of suspense: will So Lai-chen sleep with Chow Mo-wan? will they leave their spouses and marry each other? But the suspense is never resolved, and Wong leads us to another level of drama where the reference to Hitchcock becomes really intriguing. In *Vertigo*, Scottie (James Stewart) attempts to 'make over' Judy (Kim Novak) into Madeleine, the dead wife of his friend Gavin Elster, unaware that Judy *is* Madeleine. Judy then assumes the role of Madeleine, and they play at being lovers. Their affair is conducted on the level of the imagination, and when reality intrudes, the consequences are tragic.

As in Hitchcock, Wong introduces role-playing into the affair between Lai-chen and Chow. In one scene, Lai-chen plays the wife confronting her husband (a role assumed by Chow), demanding to know whether he is having an affair with another woman, and rehearsing a possible confrontation for real. In another scene, Chow confesses that he has fallen in love with Lai-chen; they rehearse their separation on the basis that Lai-chen will never leave her husband, but this role-playing is much too real for Lai-chen to bear and she breaks down, sobbing on Chow's shoulder, while he comforts her with the words: 'It's only a rehearsal.'

Hence, it is possible to discern more than one layer in the affair between Lai-chen and Chow. To begin with, there is an impressionistic layer, in which the partners 'play' with the idea of being lovers like their own unfaithful spouses, but pull themselves back from the brink of actually becoming lovers at opportune moments. Their relationship in brief encounters is sympathetic and confidential – verging on the intimate – but much care is taken to observe social decorum (even when they are by themselves in their own inner sanctum) and to keep up the impression that they are no more than neighbours and friends. Wong underscores this multi-layered dimension in the relationship in two scenes, the second a repetition of the first, but containing crucial differences in the characters' behaviour. These two scenes follow their first meeting together in the restaurant, during which the protagonists probe each other about their suspicions that their respective spouses are having an affair (quoted above). They walk home together under the night sky to the voice of Nat King Cole singing 'Te Quiero Dijiste' (also known as 'Magic Is the Moonlight'). 'I wonder how it began', Lai-chen muses. They walk into a yard engulfed in moonlight and shadow, on which stage they resume their role-playing:

LAI-CHEN: Doesn't your wife care that you come home so late?

CHOW: She's used to it. What about your husband?

LAI-CHEN: He would be asleep by now.

CHOW (making the first move): Let's not go back tonight.

(He touches Lai-chen's hand, but she recoils softly and veers away to a corner)

LAI-CHEN: My husband would never say that.

CHOW: What would he say?

LAI-CHEN: At any rate, he would not say it.

CHOW: One of us would have to say it. Who else but him?

Andy Lau, Maggie Cheung and a red bus: *As Tears Go By* (1988)

Andy Lau and Leslie Cheung in *Days of Being Wild* (1990): Andy is the introspective character, Leslie the flamboyant one

Maggie Cheung in the mood of a spurned lover: *Days of Being Wild*

Leslie Cheung and Carina Lau made for each other in *Days of Being Wild*

Knight-errant of the desert: Tony Leung Ka-fai in *Ashes of Time* (1994)

Michele Reis: portrait of a pathological angel in *Fallen Angels* (1995)

Leon Lai: portrait of a killer in *Fallen Angels*

Dancing the heartbreak tango in *Happy Together* (1997)

A male friendship in *Happy Together*: Tony Leung shakes hands with Chang Chen

Happy Together: a snapshot of Chris Doyle's luminous photography

Maggie Cheung and Tong Leung: the reluctant lovers of *In the Mood for Love* (2000)

'We will never be like them', Maggie's maxim in *In the Mood for Love*

Maggie Cheung contemplating love and betrayal: *In the Mood for Love*

2046: Faye Wong in future space and time

2046: Tony Leung thinking of *In the Mood for Love*?

is highly carnivalesque, of a kind that incorporates a Menippean discourse (after the satirical style of the ancient Greek philosopher Menippus), a style that is both comic and tragic, as Kristeva informs us:

> Pathological states of the soul, such as madness, split personalities, daydreams, dreams and death, become part of the narrative. According to Bakhtin, these elements have more structural than thematic significance; they destroy man's epic and tragic unity as well as his belief in identity and causality; they indicate that he has lost his totality and no longer coincides with himself. At the same time they often appear as an exploration of language and writing … Menippean discourse tends towards the scandalous and eccentric in language. The 'inopportune' expression, with its cynical frankness, its desecration of the sacred and its attack on etiquette, is quite characteristic.[7]

Judging by the pathological states of his characters' souls, Wong's Menippean discourse has been clear from the start. From *As Tears Go By* to *Days of Being Wild* to *Ashes of Time*, his characters are chronically pathological. Fly (Jacky Cheung) in *As Tears Go By* is practically on the verge of madness; Yuddy has an Oedipal complex that leads him to persistent womanising in *Days of Being Wild*; Brigitte Lin is a split yin-yang personality in *Ashes of Time*; and Lin basically reprises the split personality in *Chungking Express* as the faux blonde with dark glasses who takes off her wig at the end of her episode. Death is a constant, as are daydreams and nightdreams. Maggie Cheung is frail in *As Tears Go By*, is overwhelmed by lovesickness in *Days of Being Wild* and in *Ashes of Time* (she also daydreams in *Days* and dies in *Ashes*). In addition, there is amnesia, blindness and muteness. Though *Chungking Express* and *Fallen Angels* are much lighter works, evincing the comic side of the Menippean discourse, their characters are no less pathological. In fact, *Fallen Angels* is a particularly substantive model of structural and character pathology because it has even more pathological episodes and carnivalesque scenes of death (carnivalesque in the manner of parody, expressed in both a serious and funny way) than seems possible in a Wong Kar-wai movie.

We might examine these pathological episodes as they relate to each of the 'fallen angels':

- Leon Lai's killer is prone to memory loss. His apparent coolness hides not only his lack of human feelings but also his tendency or willingness to forget. This is illustrated in two episodes: the minibus episode, where he meets an old school chum (right after a killing), who actually calls him by his name 'Wong Chi-ming'[8] but whom he only vaguely recalls; and the McDonald's episode, where he meets Karen Mok's 'Blondie', an ex-girlfriend whom he has entirely forgotten. Both episodes attest to his pathological state of wilful amnesia. The original title of the song associated with the killer, 'Karmacoma' (by the group Massive Attack, rearranged by Wong's musical team of Frankie Chan and Roel Garcia), perfectly captures the character's pathology. Wong's characteristic step-printed slow motion presents the hitman walking zombie-like to his kills as if in a coma, which has arrested his karma. It is a condition that is both an occupational requirement and a hazard that seems voluntary or self-imposed. His occupation also means that he must assume a fake identity (he shows his schoolmate a photograph of a black woman and a child, who function as his 'family'), and keep an emotional distance from women. Both afflictions eventually wear him down, which he resolves by death (this being the only possible means of releasing his karma).
- Takeshi Kaneshiro's mute stopped talking at the age of five, but he 'speaks' to us through monologues. He lives and sleeps with his old father in a room in the Chungking Mansion hotel of which his father is the care-taker. We learn from his monologue that an ice-cream truck killed his mother. Our suspicion that his muteness is a strategy for avoiding interacting fully with the world can be traced to the absence of the mother, another Oedipal urge that accounts for the antisocial behaviour of Wong Kar-wai's characters (cf. the Ah Fei Yuddy's rebelliousness in *Days of Being Wild*). Wong, however, shows a benign facet of pathology in this instance: the father-and-son relationship is, on the whole, free of psychological complexes, and their episodes together stress the theme of bonding and camaraderie, touchingly conveyed in the episode of the mute's playful videoing of his father to mark his sixtieth birthday, accompanied by the Taiwanese pop number 'Thinking of You' (sung by Chyi Chin); and the episodes in which the mute breaks into shops and hawker

Wong then repeats this scene, going back to the beginning where Lai-chen and Chow walk into the stage of light and shadow:

> LAI-CHEN: Doesn't your wife care that you come home so late?
>
> CHOW: She's used to it. What about your husband?
>
> LAI-CHEN: He would be asleep by now.
>
> (At this point, Lai-chen begins to flirt with Chow, her manner assuming a coquettish demeanour. But her smile soon fades, and she turns away from CHOW, unable to be the one who makes the first move)
>
> LAI-CHEN: I can't bring myself to say the line.
>
> CHOW: I understand. What happened has happened. It doesn't matter who says it.

This repetition is extremely subtle on several counts. It introduces the motif of role-playing straight away without Wong setting it up beforehand. There are no explanations as to why Lai-chen and Chow have decided on this role-playing, and we are not sure whether or not Wong is playing a trick on us. Are the two scenes illusionary? A dream-time? Could it be that the whole affair between Lai-chen and Chow is an illusion? A little dream that might fade? On the other hand, if we accept the repeated scenes at face value – that is, on the level of role-playing – the affair is just a pretence, a charade that eventually goes wrong because it turns into a real affair and the fiction ends. Are Chow and Lai-chen preparing for the time when their affair becomes real? Just as they are preparing to confront their respective spouses about their infidelity (and thereby allowing them to take the moral high ground by only playing at being unfaithful)?

No matter how we see it, this layer of role-playing ushers us into the heart of the affair, with Lai-chen and Chow 'playing' as each other's spouse. In the next restaurant scene, for example, Lai-chen asks Chow to order for her, because she wants to know what his wife likes to eat. He in turn asks her to do the same. There is a delicious moment when Chow puts mustard on the beefsteak that he has ordered for Lai-chen: 'Is it too hot for you?' She takes a bite and grimaces: 'Your wife likes it hot.'

The motif of role-playing proved to be a difficult task for the actors. According to Wong, he had 'big arguments' with Tony Leung and Maggie

Cheung over how to play their characters. As Tony Leung describes it, he and Maggie Cheung were playing 'double roles':

> On the one hand, we were playing a husband and a wife, and on the other hand, we were playing a paramour and his mistress. In the beginning, we didn't know that our partners were having an affair, our identities were a husband and wife married to others. Then we developed a relationship and we became a lover and his mistress, which were the roles of our partners! We were playing two roles at the same time. This makes it different from all our previous roles.[7]

But role-playing added a dimension of complexity to what might have been a mundane story about marital infidelity, and the actors rose to the occasion despite the novelty of the challenge, conveying the subtleties of their roles beautifully. Leung's performance won him the Best Actor award at both the 2000 Cannes Film Festival and the Hong Kong Film Awards, while Maggie Cheung was overlooked at Cannes but recognised by the Hong Kong Film Awards. Cheung captures Lai-chen's moral dilemma in her effort to remain true to her marriage rather than succumb to her obvious attraction for Chow Mo-wan — an endeavour, underlined by her watch-words, 'we will never be like them', that turned her into the soul sister of the wife (played by Wei Wei) in *Spring in a Small Town*.

Wong compounded his actors' difficulties by instructing them to 'reveal themselves', to 'play as you are' and not just play the roles of the 'other half'.[8] In other words, Wong wanted a third dimension to the double roles. Infidelity was an excuse for Chow and Lai-chen to release their 'dark sides', as Wong put it. But both players were perhaps too decent to show their 'dark sides', and it remains a moot point as to how far they were able to realise Wong's vision. Leung may have attempted to play Chow as a vengeful man seeking payback for his wife's infidelity by having an affair with So Lai-chen,[9] but the result is more of a sympathetic wimp and loser: the archetypal weak male hero in the tradition of Chinese romantic melodramas (his pre-cursors being both the sick husband and the lover who fails to run away with his friend's wife in *Spring in a Small Town*). Chow is a cuckold, doubly betrayed by his wife and by Lai-chen. The character also recalls Lai Yiu-fai and his 'victimisation' by Ho Po-wing in *Happy Together* (see Chapter 7).

Maggie Cheung, in my opinion, was more able to evince the 'dark side' of her character just by being herself: sweet and reticent, cool and hot at the same time, intimating desire but forever repressing it. Cheung's persona incarnates So Lai-chen as a sadist, a kind of woman perceptively described by Proust, in *Remembrance of Things Past* (where she is manifested as Mlle Vinteuil), as

> creatures so purely sentimental, so naturally virtuous, that even sensual pleasure appears to them as something bad, the prerogative of the wicked. And when they allow themselves for a moment to enjoy it they endeavour to impersonate, to identify with, the wicked, and to make their partners do likewise, in order to gain the momentary illusion of having escaped beyond the control of their own gentle and scrupulous natures into the inhuman world of pleasure ... It was not evil that gave her the idea of pleasure, that seemed to her attractive, it was pleasure, rather, that seemed evil.[10]

A sadist of So Lai-chen's kind, in the words of Proust, is

> an artist in evil, which a wholly wicked person could not be, for in that case the evil would not have been external, it would have seemed quite natural to her, and would not even have been distinguishable from herself.[11]

So Lai-chen's sadism is artistry in evil that denies her and her partner (Chow Mo-wan) the sensual pleasure of sex so that she remains free of the taint of the wicked woman. Her husband betrays her but she will not betray her husband. All such contradictions are reflected in the *cheongsams* she wears (*cheongsam* is a Cantonese word meaning 'long dress' denoting the traditional costume known in Mandarin as *qipao*): it covers up the neck and breasts but offers glimpses of the thighs through side slits – in other words, the woman can be modest and seductive at the same time. The *cheongsam* denotes also that the evil in So Lai-chen is external; it stems from the husband's betrayal and his affair. Wong, however, was not interested in making a moral fable in the manner of Fei Mu in *Spring in a Small City*: 'I would rather have my actors go through both sides of an affair', a comment that rationalises, to an extent, the concept of role-playing. But Wong's idea of counteracting the role-playing through his demand to 'play as you are' imposes a constrictive coating on his actors, like the *cheongsams* that Maggie must wear (which require a slim silhouette and erect posture to carry off).

Empathy in Betrayal

Here, Wong handles role-playing for the first time in depth – it is a minor motif in *Chungking Express* (Faye Wong assuming the role of Tony Leung's girlfriend), in *Fallen Angels* (Takeshi Kaneshiro's various guises of night-time occupations) and even in *Happy Together* (Leslie Cheung playing or sending up his 'female' persona). Wong's development of the whole concept in *In the Mood for Love* entails a convoluted cycle of the actors playing roles (as husband and wife, as paramour and mistress) and then subsuming these roles to be 'themselves' (whatever that means), a technique that Wong claims to have learned from Julio Cortázar.[12] Be that as it may, identities tend to become muddled and the affair itself assumes qualities of the pseudo-metaphysical. The combined effect of all these layers produces an underlying enigma, a core of mystery and ambiguity, the ostensible secret that Chow whispers into the hole in the wall of the Angkor Wat ruins at the end of the film. The mystery or ambiguity of the film can be interpreted as a kind of impasse in Wong's career up to this point, being more a result of the circumstances of the film's production: the fact that he was piecing together material for more than one story and was working on more than one film. *In the Mood for Love* is the sum total of an idiosyncratic creative process that has its advantages and disadvantages, and in some ways shows the process in danger of heading towards a dead end.

The deleted scenes in the DVD releases of the film, published in France and by Criterion in the United States, I believe show the extent of this impasse, although they were meant to demonstrate how Wong tried to flesh out the affair with more clarity than he allowed in the actual released version. For example, a scene shows that Lai-chen and Chow did make love inside room 2046 during their hotel rendezvous, which resolves the suspense of whether they slept together, but the scene changes not only the tone of the film but also the nature of Lai-chen's character (her 'evil' would now become intrinsic to her). There is an alternative ending in which the lovers meet by chance in Cambodia four years later and become reconciled to the reality that their affair is over, after which Chow Mo-wan whispers his secrets into the hole. Again, this changes the tone of the original ending as well as Chow's character, in the sense that it makes him more a disappointed, failed lover whispering sweet nothings into a hole on the wall.

Then, there are several scenes that take place in 1972 illustrating how much the characters have changed: Chow sports a rakish moustache with a floozy good-time girl in tow as he returns to Hong Kong from Singapore, while Lai-chen is a prim housewife with a child. Wong originally intended to end the film in 1972, but it is difficult to see how leaving these scenes in the film could have resolved the mystery or the secret of the affair. The deleted scenes are in themselves far too earthy to add to the mystery (some even a bit crude); they push the film towards an emotional blockage, and were rightly deleted in my view.

Hence, the mystery remains embedded in the film, but more in the shape of an idol of the theatre, symbolising a systemic flaw in the storytelling, rather than a muse that pacifies the audience's bewilderment. Having said that, Wong achieves an atmosphere of mystery through composition and *mise en scène*. We often see the backs of people, and some characters are never shown (for instance, Chow's wife and Lai-chen's husband); sometimes they are half-glimpsed, or heard but not seen. We see the protagonists as if we are outside looking in through the curtains, like bystanders eavesdropping on private conversations. We see them disappearing around the corner, or hurrying down a corridor or staircase. An oval window through which we see the hotel reception desk where Chow's wife works shows us only a rack of hotel brochures and postcards, not Mrs Chow herself. The red curtains billowing in the wind indicate Mr Chow in his hotel waiting for his rendezvous with Lai-chen.

This is Wong's aesthetic edge of mystery. His off-centre framing and composition, complemented by his editing style of jump-cuts and elliptical cutting, recall the paintings of Pierre Bonnard and Edouard Vuillard, two artists of the Nabis group active in the late 19th century, who achieved a sense of mystery in their studies of everyday life set in the enclosed spaces of interiors. In these paintings, we often see figures only from the back or squeezed into a corner (Vuillard's *Interior* [1889] and *Mother and Child*

[1899]), or from a distance in another room in the background, framed by the doorway in the foreground (Bonnard's *Interior* [1898]). Interior spaces are cropped in curious ways into halves and rectangles (Bonnard's *Man and Woman* [1900]). Bonnard went so far as to crop the torsos of his figures, as in his *Nude in Bath* (1935), where only the legs of the bather and the lower half of a woman's body are shown. Similarly, in Wong's film, we see bits and pieces of people. This is the Hong Kong of shared apartments where space is tight, and each person is pressed for room.

There is no denying that as an aesthetic achievement the film is wholly irresistible, because of the appealing sheen of its production design and the enthusiasm for nostalgia. Wong here re-creates the past as a time when people believed in love. Tony Leung and Maggie Cheung's walk down the deserted alleyways of 1960s' Hong Kong (re-created in Bangkok) is a reprise of the Antonioni-esque walks of Andy Lau and Maggie Cheung in *Days of Being Wild* – but the mood has changed. It is no longer one of desolation so much as nostalgic romance.

On mood and nostalgia, Wong in fact takes as his aesthetic model the stories of the novelist Liu Yichang, who is, like Wong himself, a Shanghainese living in Hong Kong, though at least two generations removed (Liu was born in 1918 and came to Hong Kong in 1948). Wong quotes several passages from Liu's novella *Duidao*, translated into English under the title of *Intersections*, and first published in Chinese in 1972 (the Chinese title actually refers to *tête-bêche*, the practice in philately of printing stamps upside down relative to each other). Liu's story features two characters: a young Hong Kong woman and an elderly Shanghainese migrant, two complete strangers whose paths cross in parallel intersections, preoccupied with their own thoughts and dreams as they move around the streets of Hong Kong in the early 1970s. The young woman daydreams of her future, and the old man thinks back to his past in Shanghai. Eventually, they come together by chance, sitting next to each other in a cinema, but their separate dreams and destinies keep them apart and ensure that they will remain strangers.

Wong quotes several passages from Liu's story as epigraphic intertitles. These passages refer to the old man's nostalgia for Shanghai and his regrets for the past as he sits inside a Malaysian restaurant (he also reminisces about his past life in Singapore, the original inspiration for Wong's Singapore-set scenes). Liu's novel is essentially without plot and written as a mood piece in the stream-of-consciousness manner, denoting his character's memory and nostalgia. One of Liu's themes is time. There is a line from an earlier Liu novel, *Jiutu* (*The Drunkard*), published in 1962, which sums up the concept of time as lost opportunity for realising love and happiness, but yet time persisting as an everlasting source of nostalgic memory, of vicarious happiness: 'Time is never tired, the long needle hopelessly chasing after the short needle, and happiness is a wanderer, pacing back and forth behind the equals sign of an equation.'[13] As Liu sees it, it is Time rather than any human agency of change that makes change perceptible and emotional. Everything changes through time, particularly the environs for his protagonists, who move from Shanghai to Hong Kong to Singapore and back to Hong Kong, where, over the decades, the city changes (buildings are torn down, skyscrapers go up, people pour in, law and order deteriorates, trends and styles change, and so on).

Wong derives from Liu the idea of nostalgic mood and of time as a denominator of change. Wong's original idea, which he discarded, was to chart the changes over a ten-year period from 1962 to 1972. As it is, he decided to end his film in 1966, a time when Hong Kong was thrown into chaos as a result of riots inspired by China's Cultural Revolution (to which there is a reference in the film). Wong noted that he was interested in the idea of showing change through the changes in the characters themselves.[14] Hence, repetition as a signifier of change becomes a motif throughout the film, where once more Wong reinforces the notion that every repetition is not the same:

> The music is repeating all the time, and the way we see certain spaces, like the office, the clock, the corridors, it's always the same. We try to show the changes through minor things, like the clothes of Maggie ... details in the food, because for the Shanghainese community, it's very precise food at certain seasons. Actually, the food is telling you that it is May, it is June, or that it is July ...[15]

For a melodrama about love and romance, there are a lot of scenes of Tony Leung and Maggie Cheung eating, and discussions over and about food, which somehow makes the film very Chinese perhaps, but this is another motif derived from Liu Yichang. Wong may in fact have overdone the concept that eating together is romantic, suggesting warmth and intimacy, and that preparing food for someone is an important sign of caring for that person. But the real theme behind all that food is nostalgia: the different types of food being eaten at different times and seasons mark not only time but a remembrance of time. Do we not often think of what we have eaten in the past? The beefsteaks, the pork chops, the thermos flasks of congee and won ton noodles, all the takeaways, the food we cook, the sesame syrup, the rice cooker stir our fond memories of the past as much as do the exposed brickwork, the cobblestones, the mouldy walls, the posters disintegrating on concrete pillars that we walk past day after day. Herein lies the essence of repetition.

Maggie Cheung stepping out in high heels and *cheongsam*, handbag over an arm, hair perfectly coiffured, is the single most evocative image of nostalgia in the film. She is iconic, representing wife, lover, mistress and even a mother figure. At times, her long neck, accentuated by the closed collar of the *cheongsam*, and her perfect bouffant hairstyle transform her into a vision of ancient beauty, bearing comparison with Queen Nefertiti, especially in profile. Cheung's dizzying array of *cheongsams*, ranging from plain to flowery and colourful, is the most aesthetic marker of time ever seen in cinema. It is Wong's ecstatic way of forgetting the clocks, although in fact, of all his films, this is the one that also contains the most clocks. The film simply revels in an ecstasy of elegant design (here again, the hand of William Chang is evident). Even the colours (Wong here working with a new director of photography, Mark Lee Ping-bin, who took over after Chris Doyle shot about a third of the film) are much more refined and subdued, unlike the hyped colours of *Happy Together*. The film has the look of the Shanghai posters of the 1920s and 30s that were used as calendars or advertisements for a variety of products, ranging from face powder to cigarettes, and featuring girls in flowery *cheongsams*.

Yet, for all its elegance in re-creating the past and in capturing nostalgia, the idea of change over time is marked with an iron brand that makes the film somewhat cool and distant. The key in unlocking the secret that Tony Leung whispers into the hole in the wall lies, I believe, with the Maggie Cheung character. So Lai-chen is simply too uncertain of herself, overcome by anxiety and fear of gossip that she betrays not only Tony Leung's Chow Mo-wan but herself. Fear of gossip is the overarching conceit that justifies the sense of repression hovering over the whole affair: it prevails not only in the home environment (necessitating her hiding inside Chow Mo-wan's apartment when her landlady unexpectedly returns home, where she spends the whole night playing mahjong) but also in her workplace (her boss tries to keep his own affair with a mistress hidden, but Maggie is perceptive enough so that it becomes an open secret between them).

Gossip is a subject that Wong probably picked up from Manuel Puig, who set his novels *Betrayed by Rita Hayworth* and *Heartbreak Tango* in the town of Vallejos, 'a gossipy and nauseatingly envious town'[16] that finds its spiritual equivalent in Hong Kong's Shanghainese community. In *Betrayed by Rita Hayworth*, the young hero Toto (Puig's alter ego) finds himself at the centre of a world of scandal, betrayal and gossip. The novel is told from several points of view, including that of Toto from age nine to fifteen. In Toto's cinema-infused, impressionable young mind, the actress Rita Hayworth is the consummate betrayer of men, the kind of woman who feeds a community where gossipy women form the pivot, and from whom Toto cannot extricate himself. Like Toto, we experience a similar kind of vicariousness when watching Maggie Cheung as a screen lover, though her role is different from the kind of betrayer-women represented by Rita Hayworth. Maggie betrays Tony, and if we can imagine her for a second as the oriental Rita Hayworth, we arrive at the core of the frustration that surrounds her character. What is hard to bear is that we may feel empathy in Cheung's betrayal, for in a society of gossip, Cheung resolves not to be the object of gossip even as she becomes the object of betrayal.

Leaving for her rendezvous with Tony Leung in the hotel with red curtains, Cheung is racked with doubt and fears as she climbs the staircase, so

Contortions of space through jump-cuts and clicking high heels: Maggie Cheung on her way to her assignation (*In the Mood for Love*)

that we see her ascending and then descending, ascending again, stopping at the balcony, walking down the corridor, back to the staircase and descending the stairs, before the scene settles on a static shot of Tony Leung waiting inside his room for the knock on the door. Though these scenes were inspired by similar scenes from the Zhou Xuan movie *An All-Consuming Love*, the vision of Maggie Cheung ascending and descending the staircase in quick, indistinct, staccato movements serves equally to remind us of Marcel Duchamp's *Nude Descending a Staircase* (1912) or Gerhard Richter's *Woman Descending the Staircase* (1965), and indeed Cortázar's 'Instructions on How to Climb a Staircase', a story in his anthology *Cronopios and Famas*, which contains a description of a staircase in an imaginary, contorted space, where the floor

> bends in such a way that one part rises at a right angle to the plane formed by the floor and then the following section arranges itself parallel to the flatness, so as to provide a step to a new perpendicular, a process which is repeated in a spiral or in a broken line to highly variable elevations.[17]

The shape of the staircase is 'incapable of translating one from the ground floor to the first floor'. Wong's method of filming the sequence transmits Maggie's overwrought state to us, the space of the staircase contorting her mind even as she is climbing it, the cutting of the scene accentuated by jump-cuts and the clicking of her high heels, an apt illustration of this contortion.

We do not finally see Maggie climbing up to the first floor: the burden is perhaps too much for us as well. Instead, Wong transfers us to another state of mind – this time to Tony Leung, waiting patiently inside his room for the knock on the door. When it comes, we feel, as Leung does, a sense of satisfaction. The next shot is the corridor with red curtains. Maggie comes out of the room. After some preliminary dialogue, Tony says, 'I didn't think you'd come' to which Maggie replies, 'We won't be like them. See you tomorrow.' She walks down the corridor, as the camera pulls back to emphasise the red curtains. She then stops, in a kind of mock-freeze, a stylistic device to signal the entry of the waltz from 'Yumeji's Theme' (the theme associated with Maggie and Tony) and the transition to the next sequence – a montage of scenes showing Maggie and Tony happy together inside room 2046, the only time we see them in a state of near bliss. But happiness is a wanderer, pacing back and forth behind the equals sign of an equation. The final equation is obviously not that of Maggie and Tony, and, vicariously, neither is it that of Maggie and us. The heart changes, reality overcomes us, we are betrayed, but the worse of it is that we know it through our imagination, and we are not spared the actual sensation of change.

Nine

Wong's Time Odyssey: *2046*

Back and Beyond

The extraordinary circumstances of the making of Wong's latest opus and his eighth feature, *2046*, are now the stuff of legend. Wong apparently spent five long years making the film, thus establishing a new record in his own method of free-thinking, time-extensive and improvisatory film-making. *2046* is the one film in Wong's career that has preoccupied the director for the longest period of time. Wong pointed out that he had conceived the project as early as 1997, intending it to be a film about the implications of Hong Kong's return to China and a rumination about whether there are 'things that remain unchanged over time'.¹ The 1997 connection ostensibly places *2046* with *Happy Together*, Wong's most explicit treatment of the 1997 subject. Wong meant the title to be a reference to the last year of the fifty-year deadline in which China had promised that there would be no change in Hong Kong's political and economic system after the transfer of sovereignty from Britain to China on 1 July, 1997. Denying that he had anything political in mind, Wong insisted that his chief interest was in developing his characters and seeing them through their personal journeys.

As a project, *2046* has itself undergone a complex evolution. Its production and story line were closely enmeshed with that of *In the Mood for Love*, as has been detailed at the beginning of the last chapter: the figure itself had found its way into the latter film as the number of a hotel room in which the protagonists Chow Mo-wan (Tony Leung) and So Lai-chen (Maggie Cheung) conducted secret liaisons. While shooting *In the Mood for Love*, Wong maintained to his financiers that he was simultaneously working on *2046*, and it is only with the final release of this film to the public that its ongoing nature becomes evident. Wong now refers to it as the final part of his 1960s trilogy, beginning with *Days of Being Wild* and connecting to *In the Mood for Love*.[2] As such, the seeds of *2046* were probably sown even further back in Wong's career – to the start of the 1990s when Wong had envisioned *Days of Being Wild* as a two-part epic. Time and circumstance have allowed Wong to deliver a trilogy instead.

Describing *2046* as a 'summing up', Wong adds that he would not henceforth make any more films 'about love in the 1960s'.[3] From the chronological development of the narratives in the three films, there is indeed a case to be made that *2046* is the summation of the trilogy. *Days of Being Wild* takes place between 1960 and 1962, while *In the Mood for Love* covers the period from 1962 to 1966, and *2046* encompasses the last half of the decade, unfolding over the period from 1966 to 1970. However, Wong himself perpetuates a riddle about the trilogy by refusing to acknowledge the connection between the narratives of the three stories, instead advising viewers to see the films as separate stories. 'I consider *2046* to be a continuation of *In the Mood for Love*', Wong says, but, in the same breath, asserts, 'It's another story, about how a man faces his future due to a certain past.'[4] In so far as the production method of *2046* reflects his past history as a film-maker, the film may also be about Wong himself.

In prolonging the production period of *2046* over so many years and working on the project right down to the wire, thereby causing a last-minute delay to the showing of the film at the 2004 Cannes Film Festival in which it was to be a competing entry, Wong was certainly pushing the boundaries of his own method. Perhaps he had wanted to recapture the spirit of his last success at Cannes when he had similarly worked on eleventh-hour additions to *In the Mood for Love* – though without causing delays – hence rousing anticipation and expectation for the film (the Cannes jury awarded it two prizes). This time, however, Wong's delays engendered criticism and the film failed to win a prize. When it was eventually shown, it was clear to many that it was still a work in progress, and this is borne out also by the fact that once back in Hong Kong, Wong continued working on the film in the months leading to its final September release in Hong Kong and Mainland China. Preoccupied with getting the composite visual effects of a contemporary and a futuristic Hong Kong just right, he was at the same time re-edit-

ing the film. In August, the Hong Kong press made much play about Wong's
decision to shoot additional scenes with his Japanese leading man Takuya
Kimura, who had previously complained about the director's style of shooting his film in fits and starts, and was rumoured to have either walked out or
been fired (Kimura was also reportedly consternated to find out that his role
had shrunk).

Despite the film's prolonged production, the finished work, as represented by the 129-minute version released in Hong Kong (assuming that
this is the definitive version),[5] reaffirms Wong's status as the pre-eminent
film director of his generation in the Hong Kong cinema. Though the film
represents several landmarks for Wong (his first feature film shot in the
scope format, his most expensive feature and the longest in running time,
and the one with the most dialogue), it is classic Wong Kar-wai, in that it is
typically character-driven, lavish and atmospheric. Far from being self-
indulgent, 2046 is the most subdued and thus the least flashy of Wong's
works (even taking into account the framing scenes of a futuristic metropolis re-created through CGI, which actually constitute only a minor part of
the film). As with so many of his works, it is invariably elegiac in tone, over-
laden with a pervasive sense of sadness, fatalism and resignation, though
the mood is soothed by Wong's impeccable artistry and good taste. The
essence of the film is people's emotional reaction to change as it takes effect
over time, a delayed reaction that hits as change becomes apparent.

The motif of delayed reaction is sustained throughout the film, as Wong
repeatedly shows characters slowly overcome by the pain of separation or
loss of love. It is also the main subject of the film's science-fiction episode
where androids assume human feelings through a delayed reaction. 'If you
affect them and they want to cry, it won't be until tomorrow when the tears
start to flow,' a minder explains. In the main narrative itself, all the key
characters, with the exception of Tony Leung's Chow Mo-wan, shed tears
copiously. Chow has clearly inherited the mantle of heartbreaker from
Leslie Cheung's Yuddy in *Days of Being Wild*. As with Yuddy, Chow's character tussles with the interplay of time and emotion. But in the case of Chow,
Wong has added the variation that over time, change hardens the emotion —
the premise of 2046 being that the more time extends into the future, the

Carina Lau, a figure from the past projected into the future

more emotion is delayed. Wong does not suggest that emotion has been entirely obliterated. Chow after all is a survivor, while Yuddy is not. Chow may personify hardened emotion, yet he is not a cold, heartless character: it is just that his emotion is buried too deep within himself to flow out freely. And he charms everyone else to tears — which is the Puigian conceit from *Days of Being Wild* that Wong has applied to Chow Mo-wan.

The connections with *Days of Being Wild* are clearly discernible through the characters. Carina Lau's Lulu/Mimi from *Days* reappears in 2046; Maggie Cheung's So Lai-chen makes only a cameo appearance, a figure recalled in black and white in Chow's memory. But there is another So Lai-chen in 2046: a mysterious Mandarin-speaking black-clad woman from Phnom Penh, played by Gong Li, named Su Lizhen (the Mandarin pronunciation of So Lai-chen). Chow's meeting with Su Lizhen and the coincidence of the name causes him to recall his past and to speak of Maggie Cheung's So Lai-chen to Gong Li's Su Lizhen. One character with no relation to the other is linked by the coincidence of sharing a name, and feeling the same emotion for Chow Mo-wan. As for Chow Mo-wan himself, is he the same character as the mysterious gambler that Tony Leung plays at the end of *Days of Being Wild*? One Hong Kong film critic, writing under the pen name of Di Shiwen, thinks so, and claims therefore to have resolved the inherent riddle in Wong's trilogy that has bothered him for more than ten years. To this critic, the story, characters and the dialogue of 2046 can be sourced to *Days of Being Wild* and *In the Mood for Love*.[6]

Tatsuya Kimura, the Japanese time traveler with a secret

Whether or not Chow Mo-wan is the same character in *Days of Being Wild*, he is definitely the same man from *In the Mood for Love*. The narrative continues Chow's story from where it tapers off in that film, as he whispers his secrets into a hole in a wall of the Angkor Wat ruins. *2046* opens with a shot of a black hole, the camera pulling back to reveal that it is grandly ornamented with a feline-striped plush covering, a strikingly feminine symbol that Wong invokes with a hint of immodesty and voyeurism. Wong treats it in the first instance as a time tunnel that sucks in travellers. He leads us into the fantasy world of science-fiction, cutting directly from the hole to a shot of a futuristic mystery train as it plunges through the hole. The passenger on the train is Takuya Kimura (his character, essentially unnamed in the film, is referred to in the printed synopsis as 'Tak' and will be so referred to in the text), whose voice it is we hear offscreen in the first of Wong's typical monologues, as, speaking in Japanese, he informs us that 2046 'is a place where one can recover lost memories because nothing ever changes'.

Tak is, in fact, coming back from 2046. Curious that anyone could ever leave 2046, a minder on the train asks Tak, 'Can you tell me why you left?' He gives a vague reply about the hole – how in the old days, people would climb a mountain, find a tree and carve a hole, into which they would whisper their secrets and then cover it up with mud so that no one will discover them. Though the reply is poetically abstruse, Wong signals that he will in fact develop further the conceit of the secret linked to an illicit affair that he had introduced in his last film. Wong most likely took the conceit from

Japanese author Osamu Dazai's novel *The Setting Sun*, in which a major character commits suicide and leaves behind a note confessing his 'secret' to his sister – the secret being that he was in love with the wife of a painter. The sister has her own 'secret' (her affair with a married writer), and it is this faculty of keeping secrets which, the heroine believes, sets man apart from animals. The 'secret' of Chow's affair becomes a sort of metaphysical back story in 2046 which is evoked by the hole; but the hole raises a persisting enigma. As Chow muses later in his own monologue: 'I once fell in love with a woman and wondered whether she loved me or not.' Tak himself voices this same line in his own affair with Faye Wong's character.

Chow Mo-wan is connected to Tak and Faye Wong (her character is named Wang Jingwen) because he is himself a guest at the Oriental Hotel, having been attracted to it by the room 2046, which reminds him of his affair with So Lai-chen. From his science-fiction introduction, Wong brings us back to real time, or real time as it exists in Chow's memory: the scene of his last meeting in Singapore with Gong Li's Su Lizhen, who rejects Chow's proposal that she goes with him to Hong Kong. Being a gambler, her method of rejection is to draw cards with Chow: 'If you draw the high card, I go with you.' She draws the ace, and Chow returns to Hong Kong alone. It is the end of 1966, a time of riots in Hong Kong. The bulk of the film is given over to Chow's relationships with several women (principally Carina Lau's Lulu, Zhang Ziyi's dance-hall girl and Faye Wong) as he leads the life of a struggling writer, trying to make ends meet by writing pulp fiction in vari-

Encounter in 2046

ous genres: martial arts, sex, and science-fiction. Chow is ensconced in room 2047, though he originally wanted to stay in room 2046. The first woman he meets in Hong Kong, on Christmas Eve 1966, is Lulu. Their dialogue in this chance encounter in a nightclub is nostalgically evocative.

LULU: Have we really met before?

CHOW: You once performed in Singapore, didn't you?

LULU: Yes.

CHOW: You're called Lulu.

LULU: That was my name before, not now.

CHOW: What are you called now?

LULU: Why should I tell you?

(She starts to walk away, but stops and turns back)

LULU: Are you sure we've met?

CHOW: Have you really forgotten or are you just pretending? You said I was like your dead boyfriend. You also taught me the cha-cha.

LULU: Tell me more.

CHOW: You lost a lot of money gambling and became indebted. I and a group of friends pooled together some money to pay your return ticket to Hong Kong. You liked to talk about your dead boyfriend. A Chinese Filipino from a rich family. You wanted to marry him, but he died too young. He was the love of your life. Actually, I shouldn't be reminding you of such sad things in a time like this …

The nostalgia and heartache that Wong evokes here is two- or even three-fold. There is Lulu's nostalgia for her dead boyfriend, Chow's nostalgia for his encounter with Lulu in Singapore, and then there is our nostalgia for *Days of Being Wild* and in particular for Leslie Cheung's Yuddy. Chow's recounting of Lulu's story is the first direct clue Wong provides of his connection with *Days of Being Wild*, a film built on the coincidental linkages of the characters and the motif of time bringing them together. This recollection is not just a nostalgic episode but a demonstration of Wong's *mise-en-abîme*, denoting Wong's penchant for meta-criticism of his own works as well as his preoccupation with time and memory. The refrain that we hear in

Happy Together 'Let's start all over again', is effectively the motto behind this meta-criticism, and while *2046* is the summation of a trilogy, it can also be seen as a summation of Wong's seven feature films to date, all of which encompass facets of Wong's nostalgia for the past and an anxious thrust towards the future – symbolised not only by the mystery train that shuttles back and forth in time in *2046*, but also the train at the end of *Happy Together* and Takeshi Kaneshiro's bike-ride through the tunnel at the end of *Fallen Angels*.

Wong's placement of *Days of Being Wild* into the narrative of *2046* – via the person of Lulu and soundtrack recollections of the 'Perfidia' theme and the song 'Siboney' – is an official acknowledgment that the film initiated his 1960s trilogy of which *2046* is the final work; but apart from Lulu herself (and putting aside Tony Leung's character that appears at the end of the film), there are no connections with the stories of the other main characters in the film. Wong's overall strategy seems to be to disconnect as much as to connect. Chow Mo-wan is the personification of this strategy; he seems to be the key link in the chain connecting the three films of the trilogy, yet he has at best an ambivalent link with *Days of Being Wild*, where he is seen to possess his own space and nerve centre separate from those of the other characters. The character only comes into its own in *In the Mood for Love* and in *2046*. But, in my view, Chow Mo-wan is the chief protagonist of the trilogy because he typifies the soul of 1960s Hong Kong – the trilogy being as much about Hong Kong as it is about the 1960s. The time and the city represent eternal sadness, a mood that extends into time, given the history of Hong Kong as defined by the 1997 time index which guarantees no change for fifty years.

Though the overarching time horizon of *2046* is supposedly the future as determined by the fifty-year countdown from 1997, the film is firmly embedded in the 1960s. The film is therefore a time odyssey (not a space odyssey, as some critics mistakenly assume), exploring time from the future to the past, looking at the future from the vantage point of the 1960s. Though the decade has an unmistakably nostalgic significance for Wong, his depiction of the period is fundamentally tragic. Hong Kong in the 1960s was surviving on what the late Australian journalist Richard Hughes famously

called 'borrowed time', a pre-97 condition that produced a certain syndrome of fear and insecurity causing citizens to drift and wander – time as a
trope of restlessness. In the post-97 era, Wong suggests that Hong Kong
now survives on a state of changeless time, which still causes citizens to drift
and wander. The hidden political message of 2046 lies here: Wong is really
telling his Hong Kong audience that they should take the opportunity of
changeless time to reflect on themselves and their history – history being
rooted in the past which has given Hong Kong its period of changeless time
– in order to prepare themselves for the great changes that are to come after
2046. In 2046, the 1960s is seen as a time of chaos and uncertainty that
breeds a rootless man, Chow Mo-wan, who drifts to Singapore and back
again. In Chow Mo-wan, we see that love, permanence, fidelity and security
are elusive, and this is the ache that afflicts the heart of the trilogy and also
the ache that afflicts the heart of Hong Kong.

Flesh and Fantasy

Wong's insistence that we see the films in the trilogy as separate stories is
justified in the differences that are present in the characterisation of Chow
Mo-wan (and indeed in the characterisation of So Lai-chen in her transition
from *Days of Being Wild* to *In the Mood for Love*). Chow's change of character
from *In the Mood for Love* to 2046 is quite stark: he now sports a dandyish
moustache and is an inveterate womaniser and peeping tom, quite a contrast
from his persona in the previous film, where he is plainly a cuckold and
something of a wimp. He is the pivot of 2046, constituting the core of the narrative that interplays the factors of time and emotion in Chow's affairs with
women. Time has clearly transformed Chow Mo-wan. His affairs with So Lai-
chen and Su Lizhen have marked him, making him defensive in his relationships with women back in Hong Kong. His various affairs in 2046 are a rake's
progress of flesh and fantasy.

Chow's encounter with Lulu is extremely brief. Essentially, Lulu serves to
introduce the setting of the eponymous number, the hotel room in which she
stays and back to which Chow brings her when she passes out after a night of
revelry. On his way out, Chow notices the familiar number: 'If I hadn't met
her, I wouldn't have noticed the number and there wouldn't have been the

story of "2046".' The next day, when Chow tries to return her key, the hotel proprietor Mr Wang tells him: 'There is no one called Lulu here, there's a Mimi but she has moved out.' Chow then tries to move into the room, but is persuaded to move into 2047 because Mr Wang wants to refit 2046. 'Only later did I find out that the night before, Lulu was stabbed by her boyfriend, a drummer in the nightclub,' intones Chow in his voiceover monologue (which explains the proprietor's reluctance to rent out the room, as he needed to clean up the blood). Henceforth, Lulu is out of the picture, but she reappears later in the film – in the typically enigmatic Wong Kar-wai manner of the eternal return – apparently recovered and still dauntless in her quest to find her ideal bird without a leg. She personifies a spirit of relentlessness if not optimism.

Lulu or Mimi is the female equivalent of Chow Mo-wan's impermanent lover, and her apparent recovery also signifies Chow's own state of mind as he himself 'recovers' mentally from his affairs with the dance-hall girl Bai Ling (Zhang Ziyi), as well as the hotel proprietor's daughter Wang Jingwen (Faye Wong), who had both resided in room 2046 at separate times after Lulu's departure. Chow's relationship with Wang Jingwen is platonic, reminiscent of his affair with So Lai-chen. Like So Lai-chen, Jingwen helps Chow to write martial arts novels, effectively becoming his ghost writer, and proficiently taking over the writing of his pornographic novels as well. But she is in love with Tak, their affair going back to the early 1960s when he was working in Hong Kong as an executive for a Japanese company. Their affair

Buying time and female company: Tony Leung and Zhang Ziyi

is opposed by Jingwen's father Mr Wang (who has an aversion towards the Japanese), and because of this, Tak returns to Japan, reducing Jingwen to a nervous wreck who must be hospitalised.

Before he leaves, Tak pleads with Jingwen to 'come with me' (the scene set to Secret Garden's melancholy 'Adagio', which Wong ordered to be played on the set while shooting all the love scenes between Kimura and Faye Wong).[7] 'Do you love me or don't you?' he asks. 'Though I am afraid to ask, I must know,' and a long interval passes before Jingwen responds, but only with a tear rather than words: here again is the motif of the delayed response, where time is a determinant of emotion, where a moment of opportunity is lost in which to declare one's love. At this point, Wong jump-cuts to a point after Tak's departure before we actually hear him say 'Sayonara' and take his leave of the woman he loves, an editing technique used to emphasise the dialectic of time and emotion. Because it is delayed, the emotion is felt more deeply – and delivered here by Faye Wong's tears. In fact, throughout the film, all the leading ladies – Zhang Ziyi, Carina Lau and Gong Li – shed tears beautifully at key moments to reinforce the notion of delayed emotion, this being the single most wondrous achievement of Wong Kar-wai's direction of 2046.

As Jingwen temporarily vacates room 2046, we move into the next episode of Chow's affair with Bai Ling, who has occupied the empty room. It is in this episode that the rake in Chow Mo-wan is fleshed out and exposed before our eyes, as he is transformed into a doppelgänger of Yuddy, albeit with a moustache. Wong's inspiration for the character is the autobiographical figure in the fiction of Osamu Dazai rather than the hero of Manuel Puig's *Heartbreak Tango*. Nevertheless, Wong underscores the connection to Yuddy (inspired by Puig) by repeating several shots of Chow looking into the mirror while combing his hair, deliberately recalling Yuddy doing the very same thing. Chow's affair with Bai Ling is eerily reminiscent of Yuddy's affair with Lulu in *Days of Being Wild*, and Bai Ling's character is clearly Lulu's double in that both are fiery and temperamental as well as possessive. Like Lulu, Bai Ling works as a dance-hall escort, and like Lulu's affair with Yuddy, her liaison with Chow Mo-wan is characterised by sex. She is first introduced with the pumping sound of a springy bed as a couple makes love

Zhang Ziyi on the cakewalk

next door (supposedly Chow's room), which throws Bai Ling into a frenzy of anger. In the next scene set to the Latin rhythm of 'Siboney', Bai Ling appears in cakewalk mode, dressed in a dark coloured, beaded and very tight *cheongsam*, the very picture of a cool and seductive femme fatale. Bai Ling's episode brings out perfectly the dialectic of time and emotion: she is emotion to Chow Mo-wan's time. The dialogue between them after their Christmas Eve dinner date in 1967 (set to Nat King Cole's crooning of 'The Christmas Song') reinvigorates this motif as they walk the street (a recollection of the scene in *In the Mood for Love* where Chow and So Lai-chen take a stroll together after their meeting in a restaurant):

> BAI: I don't understand why you like to carry on so with women (referring to Chow's affairs and partying). If you meet one good woman, isn't she enough? Why delay time?
>
> CHOW: If only I can find one. A man like me has nothing but time. So I need to find people to meet my needs.
>
> BAI: You treat people like time-fillers?
>
> CHOW: Can't say that. Sometimes, I lend my time to others.
>
> BAI: What about tonight? Are you borrowing my time or am I borrowing yours?
>
> CHOW: Either way. The first half of the night, I borrow yours, the second half, you borrow mine.
>
> BAI: Don't give me that claptrap!
>
> (she turns away)

CHOW: (aghast with her reaction) Don't get me wrong. It never crossed my mind that we should have a relationship. If I wanted a relationship, I have other options. I just want us to be drinking pals.

BAI: Can you do it?

CHOW: It's difficult, but I can try.

BAI: All right, let's try.

The dialogue concerns the idea of borrowed time and the conceit of people as 'time-fillers'. Chow buys Bai Ling's time, giving her money each time after making love. She collects only ten dollars, a discount rate (to show that she is not like the other women that Chow has bought as time-fillers), keeping each ten-dollar note in a box under the bed. Because time is bought, their affair ends when he runs out of money and embarks on feverish bouts of pulp-fiction writing. In one such outburst of creativity, he makes up the story of '2046' as a place to which besotted men and women go in order to recover lost memories and are driven to kill by jealousy. He writes in the personalities he has met: thus Lulu, her lover the drummer (played by Chang Chen), Tak and Bai Ling find their way into the story. At the end of the film, after they have long separated, Bai Ling and Chow meet again in a restaurant. They spend the night drinking and reminiscing, and, as they leave, Bai Ling hands Chow a wad of money to pay the bill, this being the sum total of the ten-dollar notes with which he has bought her time. Chow is obviously moved. 'You once asked me whether there were anything I would not lend. I realise now there is indeed something I will never lend anyone,' he tells Bai Ling as he says goodbye (she leaves for Singapore the next day). As Chow walks away, he hears Bai Ling's lament 'Why can't we be like we were before?' Time walks away with the memory of another shattered love affair. In one of his earlier musings, Chow declares, 'Love is a matter of timing, it won't do if it's too soon or too late.'

Chow's relationships with the women of 2046 draw on this theme of either too soon or too late. His affair with Bai Ling having ended, the narrative continues his platonic relationship with Wang Jingwen, who moves back into room 2046. We see the warmer side of his personality coming through as he acts as the bridge to bring Jingwen and Tak together – since he

realises that Jingwen will never love him. To prevent the father from finding out that the lovers are corresponding, Chow receives love letters from
Tak, which he then passes on to Jingwen. On Christmas Eve 1968, Chow
brings Jingwen to his office so that she may telephone Tak. Chow writes
another science-fiction story in dedication of this love affair, which he
entitles '2047', a sequel to '2046'. Therefore, there are actually two science-
fiction stories in the film involving two sets of numbers. '2046' establishes
2046 as the place where amorous characters go in order to recover their lost
memories, while in '2047' Chow Mo-wan imagines himself as the Japanese
Tak (Wong underlining his Japanese inspiration, in particular Osamu
Dazai), who travels back from 2046 on the mystery train and falls in love
with the android – the sci-fi segment that opens the film, thus giving a fore-
flash of the film-within-a-film structure.

Now the film-within-a film assumes more substance as a fantasy variation of Chow's or Tak's affair with Jingwen, or in fact as an aspirational love
story in which Jingwen slowly falls in love with Chow/Tak. Significantly, Mr
Wang himself appears in the science-fiction story as the minder who cau-
tions Tak against falling in love. During this return journey, Tak seeks
warmth from Faye Wong's android attendant. He embraces her as the train
moves into a time zone of 1224 and 1225 (Christmas Eve and Christmas Day
in real time), and the android starts to 'decay' from the emotion acquired in
this exchange. He falls in love and wonders whether she loves him, but is
advised by the minder to abandon her. But Tak possesses a kind of power to
soften Mr Wang and another android on the train, Lulu, by whispering his
'secret' into their ears. The 'secret' turns out to be a command, 'Leave with
me'. Their delayed reactions over time to this 'secret' deliver to him the love
and happiness that he seeks.

Through this story, Chow has brought about a real melting of hearts, as
Jingwen finally goes to Japan to marry her lover with the consent of her
father. But Chow himself remains unfulfilled in his own real-time affairs.
Bai Ling falls passionately in love with him but he is unable to reciprocate,
and Jingwen could never have fallen in love with him: a case of too soon, too
late. He is haunted still by his liaisons with So Lai-chen and Su Lizhen. (In
his inebriated memory, So Lai-chen appears in black-and-white scenes

with his head drunkenly resting on her shoulder as they sit in a taxi.) If earlier in the film Chow has nothing but time, towards the end he has nothing
but memories, a man almost thriving on 'the wound of a guilty conscience'
– the maxim that sustains the handsome, womanising hero of Osamu
Dazai's novel *No Longer Human*, to whom 'the wound has gradually become
dearer than my own flesh and blood, and I have thought its pain to be the
emotion of the wound as it lived or even its murmur of affection'.[8]

Wong reaches the end of his time odyssey by interpolating the episode of
Chow's final meeting in Singapore with Su Lizhen into the film's concluding
segment which describes Chow's final meeting with Bai Ling in the summer
of 1970. Bai Ling has decided to move to Singapore and needs a favour from
Chow, which he readily agrees to. During their meeting, she tells him she had
tried to look him up on Christmas Eve 1969. That Christmas, Chow was in
Singapore trying unsuccessfully to find Su Lizhen: she may have returned to
Phnom Penh or she may be dead. He then thinks back to his meeting on the
stairs with Su Lizhen, which Wong had placed at the beginning of the film and
which he now recapitulates at the end. This little episode functions like a
short story in its own right, and it can be entitled 'The Black Widow', in the
manner of a Liu Yichang short story from his collection *The White in the Black
and the Black in the White*. Black is Su Lizhen's colour: she wears black
cheongsams and a black glove on her right hand. The glove, her legend goes,
hides a missing hand, the result of having once been caught cheating in a card
game. She is a professional gambler, and her meeting with Chow Mo-wan is
fated, in the sense that Chow was a gambler himself in his younger days,
appearing in this guise in *Days of Being Wild*, reinforcing his connection with
that film. The episode thus has the feel of another *mise-en-abîme*, function-
ing as an elegant coda in which Wong sums up the film's connections to *Days
of Being Wild* and *In the Mood for Love*.

Su Lizhen's brief encounter with Chow Mo-wan involves helping him
win back the money he had lost so that he can buy his return fare to Hong
Kong. Su Lizhen is a woman with a past, which she does not confide to Chow.
Chow, on the other hand, tells her of his past affair with So Lai-chen. 'I tried
to find So Lai-chen in her,' he says,' though I may not have been aware of it.'
'But she would surely have known,' he concludes. 'There are no substitutes

in love.' These thoughts are uttered after Chow had kissed Su Lizhen passionately when she rejects his proposal to go to Hong Kong with him. 'Take
care of yourself. If you can forget your past, remember to look me up.' He
leaves Su Lizhen in tears, just as he leaves Bai Ling later – a richly tearful
symmetry of time and emotion. The film reaches a symmetry of its own
through the image of the hole with which it closes. There are more secrets to
whisper to the hole, and the key to Chow's secrets is the refrain 'Leave with
me'. Chow's hurt and pain stems from the fact that neither Su Lizhen nor
Bai Ling leaves with him – and time walks away into the future with only
memories of affairs and brief encounters. Can time change, or can Chow
forget his own past and love all over again if he meets another So Lai-
chen/Su Lizhen? On an allegorical level, the film denotes Hong Kong's
affair with China through Chow's affairs with Mainland women: Zhang Ziyi,
Faye Wong, Gong Li and Dong Jie (playing Faye's younger sister who has a
brief fling with Chow). But Hong Kong, having fallen into a state of changeless time for fifty years, has a long period of delayed reaction time. It will be
fifty years before the tears flow.

Coda

Hopefully, it will not take very long for the world to recognise Wong Kar-
wai's achievement in 2046. Whether seen as a singular work or in the context of the 1960s trilogy, 2046 is a historical epic about Hong Kong's sense of
loss. The sum and substance of Wong's eight feature films to date is the cinematic recovery of Hong Kong's lost memories, and 2046 is a beautiful summation of this theme. We leave the film totally spellbound by memories of
Wong's images, the mood, and the music (a more comprehensive selection
than usual: original themes from Shigeru Umebayashi, themes from Peer
Raben, Georges Delerue and Zbigniew Preisner, plus arias extracted from
Bellini's operas *Norma* and *Il Pirata*, the voices of Nat King Cole, Dean
Martin, Connie Francis, among others). Then there are the characters: Tony
Leung is a sympathetic, complex hero, both a rake and a gentleman, the
incarnation of the personalities of Yuddy and Andy Lau's introspective
cop/sailor from *Days of Being Wild*; Zhang Ziyi and Gong Li are both magnif-
icent as the Mandarin-speaking women in Chow Mo-wan's middle-life rite

of passage; Carina Lau is affectingly evocative as the epitomic presence *en abîme* of Chow's and the film's connection with *Days of Being Wild*; and Faye Wong effortlessly exudes charm and vulnerability in her portrayal of the fragile heroine. Only Maggie Cheung's presence seems cursory and unnecessary, a sign perhaps that her 'betrayal' of Chow Mo-wan and of our vicarious romantic experience of Maggie in *In the Mood for Love* (see the last chapter) is complete.

Wong's achievement in *2046* is equally the achievement of his close collaborator William Chang, the production designer, costume designer and editor. Chang is clearly indispensable in the overall aesthetic design of Wong's films and *2046* is another dazzling contribution of his talent. On the visual side, Wong continued to work with Christopher Doyle, though their collaboration here did not apparently last throughout the five years of production. *2046* may in fact have marked their final collaboration, Doyle's vision of light and shadow and his skilful way with colours being maintained by two other directors of photography, Lai Yiu-fai (the namesake of Tony Leung's character in *Happy Together*) and Kwan Pun-leung. *2046* is another Wong Kar-wai film that is impossibly beautiful to look at.

The scope aspect ratio compels a new Wong Kar-wai visual signature: characters composed close to the edges leave vast shadow and space to fill in the rest of the frame. In this way, Wong eschews the flatness of modern art for the light and shade of the old masters (it is therefore no accident and entirely fitting that Wong uses opera arias as recurrent soundtrack themes). From dark backgrounds, single characters glow like Rembrandt portraits, like Blake's tiger 'burning bright, in the forests of the night'. Characters are placed off centre to activate the space that surrounds them with mystery and depth. In this field of light and shadow, colours glow like jewels in the dark. Wong's cinematographers are almost as adept at rendering chiaroscuro as the great Caravaggio – skilfully handling light to evoke a mysterious and imaginative world in which the psychology of the characters and their relationships could be played out. The 1960s and 70s retro décor of the settings, with their hallucinatory lime greens and reds and bold geometric patterns, paradoxically make us feel situated in the future rather than the past. Flickering lights denote the passage of time, like sunlight refracted from the windows of a speeding train, or street lights flashing past as we race by in a car. In this film, light often moves: it flickers, brightens, softens or dims; it changes direction, it casts shadows: light symbolises time in its onward passage towards 2046.

The film's final CGI tableau of Hong Kong as a futuristic metropolis (over which the end credits roll) transforms the mundane into the extraordinary: the everyday sight of office buildings and train lights on elevated tracks snaking through the city take on an unusual, sci-fi quality without losing its sense of reality. Over this cityscape, a red LG logo hangs like the mask of a mystical god overlooking the city, attesting to the capitalism and commercialism that overrides time and emotion. One key credit over this future noir shot of Hong Kong is a 'Thank You' acknowledgment to author Liu Yichang, who provided the chief literary inspiration for *2046* (and also the inspiration for *In the Mood for Love*). Wong's epigraphic intertitles are drawn from Liu's novel *Jiutu* (*The Drunkard*), and the model of Chow Mo-wan, apart from the obvious candidates in the fiction of Osamu Dazai, is also clearly the first-person protagonist of Liu's novel, a world-weary, alcoholic writer scraping a living from writing martial arts and pornographic pulp fiction.

Liu's writer has relationships with various women, including a dance hall girl and the young daughter of his landlord. His precarious existence in Hong Kong in the 1960s is the result of a fundamental clash of values: writing as an art and writing as a commercial enterprise. He sees Hong Kong as a 'concentration camp' of various evils (crime, philistinism, venality, prostitution), the whole society exacting a price of emotional pain on its citizens. 'The uniqueness of Hong Kong can only be experienced through its sufferers', Liu writes, and it is through his chief sufferer, the alcoholic writer, that Liu pours out his agony and frustration at Hong Kong itself and its artistic-literary scene (including the cinema). 'I find myself in a great dilemma, not being able to use emotion in the defence of reason and even more unable to use reason to explain emotion,' his alter ego confesses. It is Liu's belief, and that of his fictional author, that the task of a contemporary writer is to pursue 'interior truth' and not to 'describe nature'.

Inasmuch as Wong's films are inspired by literary works, *2046* can be considered an adaptation of *The Drunkard*, which is considered by Hong Kong's literati as the first Chinese stream-of-consciousness novel, a genre

Characters living on the edge in the Oriental Hotel

that Wong seems particularly fond of when we remember the influences of
Puig and Cortázar on *Days of Being Wild* and *Happy Together*. Wong has dis-
tilled the influences of the two Argentinian writers by soaking up their structures, characters and conceits. Likewise, Liu's influence can be identified
through the way that Wong intimates Liu's characters from *The Drunkard* and
Intersections, as well as the structures of these novels: fragmented, dreamlike
(the fact that each of Wong's characters speak in their own languages –
Cantonese, Mandarin or Japanese – and seem able to converse with and
understand each other nevertheless accentuates the dreamlike sensation).

2046, along with *Ashes of Time*, is easily the most literary of Wong's films,
and in its portrait of Chow Mo-wan as the worldly-wise-and-weary writer,
it can be seen as a tribute to the author Liu Yichang. In *2046*, Wong Kar-wai
has heeded the moral lesson imparted by Liu Yichang's *The Drunkard*. To
paraphrase Liu, Wong makes us feel the uniqueness of Hong Kong through
the pain of his writer; he uses the motif of time to explain emotion (with
time standing in place of Liu's reason) and he uses emotion to defend time.
Above all, he pursues the interior truth of his characters at all times. Wong
Kar-wai fulfils the criteria of the artist that Liu's author was at such pain to
achieve; his achievement is all the more remarkable insofar as he could har-
ness Hong Kong and its channels of global capitalism to underwrite his
exploration of time and emotion.

Ten
Mini-Projects and Conclusion

Short Films and Commercials

In the last chapter, I said that 2046 is a film about Wong Kar-wai himself – the film as a personal journey in which Wong is travelling on his own mystery train to another point in time, pushing his art as far as it could go. In this journey, Wong has indubitably expanded his own horizons as well as those of the Hong Kong cinema. 2046 will no doubt further transport Wong to greater international recognition, bolstering his fame and his status as one of the world's most outstanding directors. Though the film has flopped at the Hong Kong box office (as is customary with Wong's films), it will no doubt do well in the rest of the world and consolidate his global reputation with more plaudits. His previous successes at the Cannes Film Festival with *Happy Together* and *In the Mood for Love* have already established him as the most honoured Hong Kong film director in the arena of world cinema.

To his detractors, Wong has depended on his world reputation in order to survive as a Hong Kong film-maker – but this is somewhat unfair. In truth, Wong has survived because of his own unique talent as a film artist and his ability to function virtually as his own independent producer. His method of film-making may be that of a fastidious artist and his image that of a perennial *enfant terrible*, but he has shown considerable business acumen in successfully financing his productions from multinational sources (2046 was financed by French, Italian, Chinese and Japanese interests) and in pre-selling his films around the world, particularly to Asian markets: China, Taiwan, South Korea, Japan, Thailand, among others. While his films are box-office poison in Hong Kong, they do make money, albeit slowly and incrementally, from foreign sales. A film like 2046 is living proof of Wong's global and pan-Asian strategy (it features stars from all the Asian territories mentioned, while the device of having these stars speak in their own mother tongues is also part of the strategy) and would place him in a good position to pursue more outward-looking productions, the dream of every Hong Kong director. Even as he was finishing *2046*, Wong had signed a joint production and distribution deal with Fox Searchlight Pictures to make English-language films.[1] Following the release of *2046*, it was announced that he would direct Nicole Kidman in a film tentatively entitled *The Lady from Shanghai*.[2]

Wong's aesthetic and stylistic achievements make his name virtually synonymous with style, and it is on this basis that Hollywood and multinational capitalist enterprises are drawn to his cinema. Wong's skills as a visual stylist have added lustre to the products of Motorola, BMW and Lacoste. In effect, this was his entry into international film-making. Though the commercials are mini-projects in comparison with his feature films, they contain all the hallmarks of the meticulous production standards and impeccable aesthetic values seen in his features. The BMW film, entitled *The Follow* and released in 2001, is a miniature Wong Kar-wai film in all respects, from the look, to the characters, to the theme. Wong's contribution is one of a series of short films in the BMW campaign, each directed by an internationally renowned director (including Ang Lee, John Woo, John Frankenheimer, Ridley Scott and Alejandro Gonzalez Inarritu). It centres on a private detective (played by Clive Owen) who pursues various jobs while driving designer BMW vehicles involving stunts and chases. In the film, Owen's detective tails a woman suspected of cheating on her husband, a movie star. The husband (played by Mickey Rourke) tries to explain his reason for the job: 'It's impossible to describe how painful infidelity is. It just rips you apart at the seams' – a classic Wong Kar-wai line in view of his preoccupation with the theme in *In the Mood for Love* and, in varying degrees, in *Happy Together*, *Fallen Angels* and *Ashes of Time*. Driving a BMW Z3 roadster as he shadows the wife, the detective recites a monologue underscoring his code of professional practice:

> You vary your distance, you stay to the rear, to the right, never more than a few cars behind. It's all about patience, percentages, timing. If you get too close, move into their blind spot. If you lose them, just keep moving, hope for the

best. Out in the open, the distance is subjective, you can let the target ride to the horizon, so long as you know their pattern.[3]

These scenes are essentially selling the product, but then Wong has his own take of the hard sell. He effectively builds up a Chandleresque mood in the monologue, which becomes ever more introspective. 'The waiting is the hard part. Your mind wanders, wondering what it would be like watching your own life from far away,' the detective muses. At the same time, Wong strives to re-create Chandler's world of sleazy bars and dark urbanscapes in modern Los Angeles.[4] Owen's detective is the modern equivalent of Philip Marlowe, who ultimately acts on his conscience even as he gives voice to his professional code, emphasising the need to keep an emotional distance. Following his target to the airport, where she checks in for a flight to Brazil, he therefore maintains a discreet distance and keeps a cool head ('If the target doubles back, never react'). He watches her in the bar where she is forced to wait when her flight to Brazil is delayed (the Brazilian origin of the wife reiterating the Latin American motif in Wong's works). He warns, 'Whatever you do, don't get too close. Never meet their eyes.'

But then he breaks his own rule. When she falls asleep, her face lying prone on the bar table, he gets close to her, looking at her exposed eyes as her dark glasses slip slightly from her face; he sees her blackened eyes and the white knight in him is aroused. The whole scene is adorned on the soundtrack by the lushly romantic song 'Unicornia' (a Latin American standard), performed by Cecilia Noël, recapitulating the loneliness of a man and a woman in a bar, and recalling Takeshi Kaneshiro and Brigitte Lin in *Chungking Express*, Leon Lai and Michele Reis in *Fallen Angels*. The song is expressive of the kind of telekinetic non-verbal communication between the two protagonists, breaching the distance and silence between them. The detective finally returns the money to his employer (the star's manager, played by Forest Whitaker), saying simply, 'I lost her'. Owen's understated performance, his tenderness, makes him an archetypal Wong Kar-wai character in the mode of Tony Leung.

Though *The Follow* has all the qualities and features of a film (it is in fact the first film that Wong shot in the scope format; *2046* is the first feature in which he uses the format), the nature of its dissemination as a streaming broadband video is a sign of the predominance of the new technology in the new millennium and the importance of the Internet in contemporary pop culture. Running all of eight minutes, the film seems to fit like a glove into the hand of the new media. Wong's elliptical style, marked by intercutting scenes of the detective's monologue as he follows the wife and the meetings with Whitaker and Rourke setting him up for 'the hire' (which is the title given to the series), plays like a poststructuralist discourse over time and memory that Internet chatters might appreciate as a true expression of online communication, combining image-making and the soliloquies of thought. In contrast, the other entries in the series (such as those by Frankenheimer, Inarritu, Guy Ritchie and the later contributions of Woo, Ridley and Tony Scott) are grandstanding action pieces that intrinsically work far better on the big screen than on computer terminals.

Perhaps *The Follow* is ultimately no more than a curiosity in Wong's oeuvre, but it is a more telling example of his post-modern artistry of intermixing streams of pop art, advertising kitsch, MTV, literary monologues and non-linear storytelling, allowing contemporary audiences an immediate sense of, and identification with, modern cross-media culture. Despite its post-modern trappings, *The Follow* is consistent with Wong's romantic inclination and penchant for a mood that looks back to the old days (in this instance, the film noir atmosphere of Raymond Chandler and the 1940s and 50s).

Wong's Lacoste commercial, released in 2002 and also viewable online,[5] features Chang Chen, wearing a red polo shirt sporting the Lacoste alligator logo, in a drowsy, dreamlike encounter with a Western woman, wearing a black polo shirt, on board a Shanghai ferry. A quick montage of scenes transports the viewer to the denouement, in which Chang puts on the black polo shirt as he stands on the roof of a building in the middle of the Pudong metropolis, the woman separately gazing on in telepathic communion. The soundtrack resounds to the music of Shigeru Umebayashi from *In the Mood for Love*, a reference point indicating that Wong's current international fame and his reputation as a film stylist are really indebted to his last film.

Working again with Chang Chen, Wong made 'Six Days', a music video for DJ Shadow, released in 2002.[6] Reportedly a fan of the turntable artist and his 'trip-hop' music, Wong produced an archetypical visual feast (shot by Christopher Doyle), giving his own slant to the song's anti-war theme ('Negotiations breaking down/See those leaders start to frown/It's sword and gun day/Tomorrow never comes until it's too late'). Wong interprets the song as a tale of betrayed love, showing the lovers (Chang Chen and the Hong Kong model Danielle Graham) making love and war with equal intensity in the three minutes and forty-one seconds running time. Betrayal is symbolised by time going backwards on a clock. – '4.27' flips to '4.26' and thereafter remains frozen – a familiar motif of time and numbers which Wong develops with the dispatch of hallucinatory memory. Chang Chen smashes and destroys all traces of '4.26' with martial arts devastation, the numbers being constantly inserted into the images, appearing as a tattoo on the sole of Chang's feet, a scratch on the mirror, wired in the light bulb. In the end, following the destruction, the numbers are broken up into constituent parts.

The dreamlike impressions of 'Six Days', and of the Lacoste commercial, are reminiscent of an earlier commercial that Wong made for the cellphone company Motorola in 1997, after the release of *Happy Together*. The Motorola commercial (hereinafter referred to as 'Motorola' for the sake of convenience), featuring Faye Wong and the Japanese actor Tadanobu Asano, which runs in a three-minute extended version, is possibly the most brilliant and beautiful of Wong's commercials (or at least of the four works discussed here).[7]

Shot by Christopher Doyle and designed by William Chang, 'Motorola' is really a visual composition – as distinct from a film or even a commercial, as Wong himself emphasises.[8] The theme is communication, or rather, as Wong presents it, the inscrutability of communication. Communication takes place in dream space and memory between a woman (Faye Wong) and a man (Tadanobu Asano), apparently her ex-boyfriend, who is recalled at the moment that Faye makes a call in the opening shots and to whom she waves goodbye in the last shots before the 'Motorola' sign rudely intrudes to remind us that the film is really meant to sell cellphone products. In between, we see Faye sitting languidly on a chair, lifting her hand as if to conjure up her boyfriend in real space, then reclining on a table, jump-cuts changing the spatial backdrops and our perspectives of her, placing her in different states of memory and recollection. These dream states are juxtaposed with images of her boyfriend, engrossed by a pinball machine and the television, showing the various stages of his neglect in their relationship; all of which climaxes in a brief shot of an imploding building. This short work shows Wong at his best, encapsulating the beautiful images with its theme of the pathology of love in only three minutes, perfectly complementing the director's vision familiar from his features.

The feature films that 'Motorola' and 'Six Days' most remind us of are *Happy Together*, because of its hyped colours and baroque sets, and *Chungking Express*, because of the incessant and repetitive movement – an essential element of the MTV style. As the short works overlap with Wong's cinematic features, is it a case of Wong Kar-wai emulating the MTV style or MTV emulating Wong Kar-wai? Certainly, there are a lot of similarities: choppy narratives, jump-cuts, scenes that loop or appear to loop, pop songs that throb to beautiful images. Wong's commercial work attests to his versatility as a filmmaker, proving that he is at home in long and short works, and as able to communicate his suite of personal motifs and obsessions in both formats. Part of the fun of watching the commercials lies in deciphering Wong's embedded clues to interpret not only the intended meanings but also the allusions to his feature films. But could there be a danger that as we decipher the signs and read the meanings in the short works, we may begin to feel that Wong's feature films themselves are only as interesting as an MTV video?

As I hope this book has shown, Wong's features have not vitiated to the level of MTV because of the contexts they invoke: their historical nexus with past eras, their identification with the times, their interconnectedness of the local with the global, and, above all, their depth of meaning and feeling. There is also no logical reason to discount works like 'Motorola', 'Six Days', and *The Follow* from critical analysis simply because of their short length and their nature as MTV-style commercials. They are a fundamental part of Wong's oeuvre, miniature models of his cinema that shore up the canon rather than detract from it.

Since 2046, Wong has made a forty-minute episode in a three-film com-
pilation entitled *Eros* (the other episodes contributed by Michelangelo
Antonioni and Steven Soderbergh). Wong's short film is called *The Hand*, a
work he shot in mid-2003 during a break in the making of 2046. The film
stars Gong Li and Chang Chen as a seasoned seductress and a tailor's
apprentice who become involved with each other. I have not been able to see
the film at the time of writing this chapter (the film was first shown at the
Venice International Film Festival in September 2004), but most critical
appraisal has indicated that it is a major work recapitulating themes of
desire, obsession and infidelity.

Conclusion

Ultimately it is Wong's eight feature films that must secure his status as an
auteur. Eight feature films is not a prolific output by the standards of Hong
Kong cinema, but it is a substantive body of work by the standards of world
cinema. Of these eight films, at least five – *Days of Being Wild*, *Ashes of Time*,
Happy Together, *In the Mood for Love* and 2046 – had involved a great deal of
time, money and energy, each film, with the exception of 2046, taking more
than a year in the shooting and post-production process. In that time a normal working director in the Hong Kong industry would have made two or
three films. 2046 of course, took five years, which is unprecedented even for
Wong. What this shows is that Wong is quite simply the best director in the
Hong Kong cinema when judged purely from the criteria of his profession.
He oversees every aspect of his productions and is a meticulous craftsman.

As an auteur, Wong's eight films form a body of work that maintains a
high level of standards and consistency of style, but his skill as a film-
maker extends to his ability, so far, to delineate each film separately as a
work in its own right. *As Tears Go By* is a typical 1980s gangster film made
untypical by Wong's style. *Days of Being Wild* is an extraordinarily bold
departure from the mainstream, a 1960s period movie that takes us through
the labyrinths of its characters' anguished hearts and minds. *Ashes of Time*
transports us to an ancient martial arts historical period, but still works as
a modern character study in the manner of *Days of Being Wild*. *Ashes* has its
own tone and rhythm, distinctly different from *Days* and from *Chungking*

Express, which is hip and contemporary. *Fallen Angels* bears comparison with *Chungking Express*, but exerts its individuality by presenting Hong Kong as a holistic entity, while *Chungking* is very much identified with Tsimshatsui and Central. *Happy Together* is set outside Hong Kong altogether, a study of angst in a gay relationship that echoes the pre-97 mood of Hong Kong. *In the Mood for Love* transports us back to the 1960s, the period of *Days of Being Wild*, recycling Maggie Cheung's character from that film; but in contrast to *Days* and *Happy Together*, it portrays a more conservative time, with its two chief characters repressing rather than expressing desire. *2046*, though a continuation of *In the Mood for Love*, is something altogether different, presenting Tony Leung's writer as a world-weary romantic who casts one eye to the past and the indeterminate future while using the other to wink at the beautiful women who cross his path.

All eight films have created a mystique around Wong Kar-wai – a mystique founded as much on a mercurial method of film-making involving improvisation and free creativity, as it is on telling stories built around abstract propositions of time and space. These methods of film-making and storytelling create a central paradox: Wong's films, in the end, seem too finely crafted to be wholly improvised. Seemingly enigmatic, even superficial in their eclecticism, like assorted biscuits in a tin, they are actually emotionally probing and historically relevant, more like fine cheeses or wines that mellow with age, revealing Wong's perspicacity of both human psychology and his insightful knowledge of Hong Kong's modern history. In fact, Wong's career may be summed up in a number of other paradoxes that demonstrate how special he really is.

The paradox of the local and the global

This book has sought to analyse Wong's films closely as the creative and instinctive response of an artist brought up in a Hong Kong environment that has always fashioned its own unique interpretation of film art and culture: making something new out of a patchwork quilt of Eastern and Western elements and a crossing of many genres. Just like Hong Kong itself, Wong's films constitute a cornucopia overflowing with multiple stories, strands of expressions, meanings and identities: a kaleidoscope of colours and identities. It is taken for granted that Wong's films provide a substitute to the crass commercial fare of most of Hong Kong cinema and to the Hollywood blockbusters that dominate the cinemas of the world, but they also give us alternative ways of looking at art cinema. Wong's cinema may be defined as asymmetric art in a way that makes it distinctive in both Eastern and Western contexts. It is much too romantic, much too emotional and ultimately much too Hong Kong to be located in the same topography of European-style high art cinema; and it is much too cool, much too genteel and ultimately much too other-worldly to be simply recognised as Hong Kong.

The best take on this paradox is to concede that Wong's cinema belongs to Hong Kong and the world. Wong's art can be said to be both local and global at the same time, his accomplishments all the more extraordinary because they are examples of contemporary localism that manifest the 'global in the local', to borrow the title of an essay by Arif Dirlik.[9] In this essay, Dirlik is concerned with the spread of global capitalism and the means of resistance to it. To Dirlik, localism spells resistance, the outcome of a historical and political struggle by groups suppressed or marginalised by modernisation. He defines contemporary localism as 'a postmodern consciousness, embedded in new forms of empowerment'.[10] I believe Dirlik's thesis affords us the most perceptive way of looking at Wong Kar-wai as a post-modern figure. In this view, Wong is really a film-maker marginalised by Hong Kong's film capitalistic forces but who has so far managed to avoid being overpowered by them. His cinema embodies variations of genre and art cinema, making his films populist and cerebral at the same time.

It is important to remember that, in his expression of local themes, Wong's career began to flourish in the 1990s following his critical breakthrough with *Days of Being Wild* (1990). The 1990s was a time of great movements and changes in Hong Kong cinema, and Wong himself was a key player. *Ashes of Time*, *Chungking Express*, *Fallen Angels* and *Happy Together* elucidate the great issues of the decade. First, there was the issue of 1997, which generated insecurity and anxiety, a crisis of identity and a pervading sense of psychological malaise affecting both individuals and families; second, there were social issues such as homosexual rights, gender inequality and crime rates; and third, issues of personality and the broader humanity, such as loneliness, infidelity and alienation also needed to be addressed. Wong's films of the 1990s leave behind an anthropological and cultural record of Hong Kong that must be treasured.

In his expression of global nuances, Wong's films make us realise that in a truly multicultural world, understanding of other cultures is an imperative and that nothing can be taken for granted. They are an expression of multiculturalism that enrich the viewing experience. Their rich aesthetic and thematic tapestries, not to mention the labyrinthine linking of separate stories, constitute a kind of eternal memory that it would be foolish to discard after only one viewing. Wong's cinema is the kind that grows from multiple viewing, challenging the belief held by some critics that one should only watch a film once. His appeal in our contemporary age is that of an artist whose works accommodate the modules of new technology and communication channels and reverberate all the more strongly because of it. In Wong's time, the cinema is only one part of a whole viewing experience; in many ways, the structures of his films and the method of his storytelling reflect the growth of the Internet, broadband and DVD – media that nurture alternative and multiple viewing options.

The paradox of the visual image and the written word

As I have tried to demonstrate throughout this book, Wong's cinema integrates literature and visual style in ways that only he has cared to see through. In his conjoining of literature and cinema, Wong paradoxically shows a love of literature that seems far greater than his love of cinema. Literature feeds Wong's faculty of image-making. He is inspired by writers such as Puig and Cortázar, Osamu Dazai and Liu Yichang to express non-linear, illogical narratives, using the word in his own distinctive manner to combine thought and image, and heighten our senses of perception. From these authors, Wong appropriates conceits, lines of dialogue and characters, refashioning them into a unique personal vision. It is remarkable that he can seemingly rely on literary conceits to construct images of breathtaking beauty (one thinks of the 'secret' that Tony Leung whispers to the hole at the end of *In the Mood for Love*, or the 'secret' correlating to the hole in *2046*; or the conceit of impossible love in a foreign country that makes *Happy Together* a visual masterpiece). To Wong, literature liberates cinema, or perhaps it would be true to say that if his films offer a balance, it is a balance between the visual image and the written word.

As a natural outcome of the literary quality of Wong's cinema, his films extend the field of film criticism, hopefully improving standards by pushing its boundaries into fallow plots of theory. To understand his films is to understand cinema as a theory of language and communication, of difference and repetition, of movement, space and time. In this regard, Wong's films are remarkably fluid and await even deeper exploration and discovery. On a personal level, revisiting Wong's films in writing this book is really to indulge in the pleasure of cinema on the one hand, and to renew the pleasure of literature on the other hand. Wong's monologues and his facility in creating small literary vignettes make him almost unique in the contemporary cinema as a director who pays as much attention to the word as to the image. But Wong's love of literature is particularly revealed in the structures of his films (whether it is the non-linear narratives, the fondness for literary intertitles or his concentration on characters), which fundamentally change our way of looking at cinema.

Ultimately, Wong would not occupy the position he does today if he was not recognised as a supreme creator of striking visuals and a master storyteller exerting an influence of his own. While there are directors who no doubt imitate and copy him, his influence is best felt in the works of those who are as idiosyncratic as he is. Korean director Lee Myung-se (*Nowhere to Hide*), the Austrian Tommy Tykwer (*Run Lola Run*), China's Zhang Yuan (*Green Tea*) and Lou Ye (*Suzhou River*), the American Quentin Tarantino (*Kill Bill, Volume 1*) and Hong Kong's Tsui Hark (*The Blade*), to name only a handful, display facets of a Wong Kar-wai sensibility in visual style and narrative organisation. It is how Wong has changed the way we view cinema that matters, and here it is his influence in shaping cinema as an experience of dream and reality that counts most.

The paradox of dream and reality

Though one comes away from a Wong Kar-wai film with a feeling of having stirred from a not too unpleasant dream, it is essentially a realistic cinema that is neither gritty nor prosaic. In this paradox, we recognise that Wong's cinema is basically psychological without being neurotic or hysterical. The final conclusion that we may draw from Wong's eight feature films to date is that he is the director who has portrayed most meaningfully the pathology of Hong Kong in the pre-97 period. (I, of course, include *In the Mood for Love* and *2046* in this cycle of eight films, although they were made after 1997: both films are set in the 1960s; one ends and the other begins in 1966, the year when violent riots erupted in the city whereby Wong anticipates the whole psychology of the pre-1997 era.) However, if his cinema mirrors the pathology of Hong Kong society in the 1990s, it does so without a sense of derision, recrimination or malice. Wong's colleagues in the New Wave have not been so kind or gentle in their cinematic treatments of the Hong Kong malaise: Tsui Hark's *The Blade* (1994), a film that followed on the heels of *Ashes of Time*, is much more vicious and unrelenting in its vision of a martial arts world as an allegory of Hong Kong's China syndrome in the lead-up to 1997; Clara Law's *Farewell China* (1990) compares with *Days of Being Wild* as a testament of Hong Kong Second Wave identity, but Law depicts more hysterically the paranoia inherent in the Chinese dream of emigration; and Stanley Kwan's *Hold You Tight* (1998), a companion piece with *Happy Together* in its expression of homosexual identity, is compromised and flawed by a patronising view of the female and the institution of marriage.

The moderate quality of Wong emerges in providing a balance between reality and dream. It has certainly something to do with the creative photography, the soundtracks working in conjunction with the camerawork, the unusual use of colours enhancing our perception, the skill of his actors and the quality of his direction – and all to do with Wong Kar-wai's imaginative rather than conventional treatment of everyday themes concerning love, infidelity and friendship. Watching his films, we are drawn into a web interweaving dream and reality. Wong's films are a dream, because they are beautiful to look at and because the purity of his characters' emotions take centre stage – and yet they also express a reality, because they harbour the pain and pathology of real human relations, and thus ring true.

The nature of dream and illusion in Wong's cinema is perhaps close to his own nature as an artist, but this is not to say that it is a form of escape from reality. There is a fatalist streak in Wong: his films often end in death and despair, but there is something uplifting if not noble about his type of despair, typically represented by the image of Tony Leung whispering secrets into a hole in the wall at the ruins of Angkor Wat in *In the Mood for Love*, and Clive Owen's words at the end of *The Follow*, 'I lost her. Don't ever call me again', or the vision of women crying majestically at the end of *2046*.

The dignity of despair in Wong's films is a kind of Zen-like recognition of the state of depression in which the Hong Kong film industry has been wallowing for close to ten years. It is a curious fact that just as his career took off from the release of *Ashes of Time* and *Chungking Express* (1993–4), it coincided with the beginning of the decline of Hong Kong cinema. Wong's career since then has progressed in contradistinction to the general decline of the film industry. It cannot be denied that his style militates against the commercial tendencies of the Hong Kong film industry and that the melancholic mood of his films is inimical to box-office success in an industry long convinced that the way to attract audiences back to cinemas is to lift their moods and to dumb down. Yet, despite the best efforts and the odd blockbuster success, the depression has not gone away, and no film has as yet comprehensively revivified the industry and brought back the golden age. In a way, the downbeat mood of Wong's films reflects the mood of the industry as it lingers on the downswing.

The decline of Hong Kong cinema is the symptom of a larger malaise with economic and political dimensions, which befell Hong Kong in the final decade of the last century. Wong is the child of the depression, not its father, and if his films are carefully designed manifestations of the depression, or of millennial disillusionment, they are nevertheless transcending works whose objective is not to alienate the audience with inertia; rather, they are a therapeutic course of treatment, making a point to entertain the audience with sensations of colour, design, movement, action and drama.

On this score, Wong is like any other Hong Kong film-maker who knows what cinema is about (he is, after all, a contemporary of directors such as John Woo, Tsui Hark, Wong Jing, Jeff Lau, Stephen Chow). After eight films, Wong has proven to be a masterful artist who both pleases the eye and makes a pitch for our emotions. Not so well known is the fact that he takes risks, both artistic and financial, simply by committing himself in a way that his contemporaries cannot match. Up to now, Wong has remained true to himself by being the kind of director who makes the films he wants to make and in his own method. He has not yet made a bad film, or an indifferent one. His career is still developing and far from reaching the end point. There will be more films, more variations, repetitions and differences that demand criticism and analysis. In making each project since *Days of Being Wild* journeys of exploration, Wong often spent incredible lengths of time completing his films, and consequently, he aggravates the industry and displeases the money men. But he is like the white knight in a Chandleresque world of dark mutterings, intrigue and betrayal – as in the world of Puig and Cortázar, the world of Murakami, of JinYong and Liu Yichang – who rides on dauntless and indomitable. We are like his fellow travellers. When Wong embarks on his next mystery train, we will do well to follow, even if he takes us to the ends of the earth.

NOTES

1 – Introduction

1. David Bordwell, *Planet Hong Kong* (Cambridge, MA and London: Harvard University Press, 2000), p. 270.

2. Ackbar Abbas, *Hong Kong: Culture and the Politics of Disappearance* (Hong Kong: Hong Kong University Press, 1997), p. 50.

3. For a very recent study in which the literary roots and influences of one of Wong's films are analysed in depth, see Jeremy Tambling, *Wong Kar-wai's Happy Together* (Hong Kong: Hong Kong University Press, 2003).

4. Author's interview with Patrick Tam, 27 March 2003, Hong Kong.

5. Michel Foucault, 'Nietzsche, Genealogy, History', in Donald F. Bouchard (ed.), *Language, Counter-Memory, Practice: Selected Essays and Interviews by Michel Foucault* (Ithaca, NY: Cornell University Press, 1977), p. 154.

6. Abbas, *Culture and the Politics of Disappearance*, p. 48.

7. Ibid., p. 16.

8. See Liza Bear, 'Wong Kar-wai', *Bomb Magazine*, no. 75 (Spring 2001).

9. Ibid.

10. Ibid.

11. See Mary Jane Amato and J. Greenberg, 'Swimming in Winter: An Interview with Wong Kar-wai', published in the online magazine *Kabinet*, no. 5 (Summer 2000), <www.kabinet.org/magazine/issue5/wkw1.html>.

12. Ibid.

13. Ibid.

14. These and other deleted scenes can be seen in the DVD editions (released by Criterion and the French distributor TF1 Video and Ocean Films).

15. Interview with Tam. Wong has claimed that he 'spent years' writing the script of *Final Victory* and that when he handed it in, his bosses demanded rewrites and revisions. See Jimmy Ngai, 'A Dialogue with Wong Kar-wai', in Jean-Marc Lalanne, David Martinez, Ackbar Abbas and Jimmy Ngai, *Wong Kar-wai* (Paris: Dis Voir, 1997), p. 101.

2 – In Mainstream Gear

1. Jimmy Ngai, 'A Dialogue with Wong Kar-wai', in Jean-Marc Lalanne, David Martinez, Akbar Abbas and Jimmy Ngai, *Wong Kar-wai* (Paris: Dis Voir, 1997), p. 101.

2. See 'Wang Jiawei Zongtan "Wangjiao Kamen"' ('Wong Kar-wai on "As Tears Go By"'), *Dianying Shuangzhou Kan* (*Film Biweekly*), no. 241 (16 June 1988), p. 24.

3. Ibid.

4. Interview with Patrick Tam, 27 March 2003, Hong Kong.

5. 'Wong Kar-wai on "As Tears Go By"', p. 24.

6. Ibid.

7. Interview with Tam.

8. 'Dudang Yimian de Wang Jiawei' ('Wong
   Kar-wai Takes Charge'), *Dianying
   Shuangzhou Kan (Film Biweekly)*, no. 244
   (28 July 1988), p. 17.

9. In Wong's original ending, Wah is shot
   but not killed. He is mentally
   incapacitated, with Maggie Cheung
   looking on silently. According to Wong,
   there were two reasons why this ending
   was cut; first, it would make the film
   too long, thus affecting its distribution;
   and second, it was felt that the audience
   would not accept Andy Lau as an idiot
   but would rather see him die. See
   'Wong Kar-wai on "As Tears Go By"',
   p. 25.

10. Interview with Tam.

11. 'Wong Kar-wai on "As Tears Go By"',
    p. 24.

12. The Chinese title, *Wangjiao Kamen*,
    which translates literally as 'Mongkok
    Carmen', is much more evenly balanced
    between the gangster and romance
    elements – 'Mongkok' symbolising the
    gangster part, while 'Carmen' evokes the
    romantic element. According to Wong,
    'Mongkok Carmen' was a different
    screenplay altogether, telling the story
    of a young detective who falls in love
    with a dance hall girl, transposing the
    Carmen plot into the Mongkok setting.
    During the shooting of *As Tears Go By*,
    several actors mistakenly thought that
    he was making the Carmen script and
    perpetuated the mistake to journalists.
    This way, the Chinese title stuck, and
    remained the film's title even though
    Wong had intended to change it before
    the release date. See 'Wong Kar-wai on
    "As Tears Go By"', p. 24.

13. 'Wong Kar-wai on "As Tears Go By"',
    p. 24.

14. Ibid.

15. Ibid.

16. Ibid.

17. See, for example, the review in *Dianying
    Shuangzhou Kan (Film Biweekly)*, no. 242
    (30 June 1988), entitled '"Wangjiao
    Kamen": Lanyong le Yingxing Xiaoguo'
    ('"As Tears Go By": A Misuse of Image
    Effects'). The reviewer, a writer named
    simply Peter, makes the point that
    although the film's particular treatment
    of images represented something quite
    rare in Hong Kong cinema, such images
    were already clichés in international
    cinema, a criticism that would be voiced
    many times over as Wong started to
    acquire more widespread recognition.

18. 'Wong Kar-wai on "As Tears Go By"',
    p. 25. Patrick Tam edited two action
    sequences, including Andy Lau's attack
    on the snooker king, while Or Sing-pui
    edited those sequences featuring Alex
    Man. Director Stanley Kwan worked on
    the post-synch dubbing of the dialogue.

19. William Chang (name in Pinyin: Zhang
    Shuping; in Cantonese: Cheung Suk-
    ping) was born in 1953 and educated at
    the New Method College, a private high
    school. After graduation, Chang sought
    work in films and was taken on by the
    female director Tang Shuxuan as her
    assistant director. He then went to
    Canada in 1973 to study film at the
    Vancouver School of Arts. On his return
    to Hong Kong three years later, he
    worked in the field of fashion design
    before making his debut as production
    designer on Patrick Tam's *Love Massacre*

(1981). Since then, Chang has worked regularly on many films, mainly as a production designer, but also as costume designer, modelling designer and editor. Apart from Wong, other notable directors whom Chang has worked with include Tsui Hark, Yim Ho, Stanley Kwan and Tony Au.

3 – Wong's Heartbreak Tango

1. In a pre-release interview with Jimmy Ngai, Wong revealed that he had planned the film as a single work but had divided it into two parts because of commercial considerations. Wong referred to the possibility of re-editing the projected two parts into a single three- or four-hour film for video release, and spoke of this future video version as his 'ideal project'. See Jimmy Ngai, 'All About "A Fei Zhengzhuan": Yu Wang Jiawei Duihua' ('All About "Days of Being Wild": A Dialogue with Wong Kar-wai'), *Dianying Shuangzhou Kan (City Entertainment)*, no. 305 (6–19 December 1990), p. 38.

2. Originally, *Days of Being Wild* was set in three time frames and locations: a fishing village in the 1930s, Kowloon in 1960 and the Philippines in 1966. Wong decided finally to delete the 1930s' sequence. See Ngai, 'A Dialogue with Wong Kar-wai'.

3. Gilles Deleuze, *Difference and Repetition*, trans. Paul Patton (London and New York: Continuum, 1994), p. 41.

4. The fable of the bird and the Chinese title *A Fei Zhengzhuan* also betray a definite connection with Lu Xun, China's greatest man of letters of the 20th century. The bird fable is possibly influenced by a line in the preface to the writer's *Huagai Ji (The Huagai Collection)*, an anthology of essays published in 1925, in which the author wrote, 'When I was a boy, I dreamed of flying in the air, but up to the present, I am still grounded on earth.' The title *A Fei Zhengzhuan* recalls one of the author's most famous stories, *A Q Zhengzhuan (The True Story of Ah Q)*, published in 1921.

5. Ngai, 'A Dialogue with Wong Kar-wai'.

6. See Tianshi, 'The Days of Being Wild: Feilübin Waijing Bari' ('The Days of Being Wild: Eight-Day Location Shooting in the Philippines'), *Dianying Shuangzhou Kan (City Entertainment)*, no. 306 (20 December – 2 January, 1990), p. 36.

7. Ngai, 'A Dialogue with Wong Kar-wai'.

8. Tianshi, 'The Days of Being Wild'.

9. The critic and film-maker Cheung Chi-sing, for example, wrote in a review that Wong was 'simply a naughty child doing as he pleases upsetting the order of the real world, relying on nothing more than his private fancies'. See Cheung, '"A Fei Zhengzhuan":Wogan Wosi' ('My Feelings and Thoughts on "Days of Being Wild"'), *Dianying Shuangzhou Kan (City Entertainment)*, no. 308 (17–30 January, 1991), p. 119.

10. Ngai, 'A Dialogue with Wong Kar-wai'.

11. Ariadne was the daughter of King Minos of Crete who helped Theseus escape from the Minotaur's lair with a golden thread. Theseus abandons her on the island of Naxos after promising to marry her. The myth of Ariadne had

symbolic meaning for De Chirico and appears as a persistent theme in many of his paintings.

12. From Eliot's 'Preludes', *The Waste Land and Other Poems* (London: Faber, 1972), p. 15.

13. Interview with Patrick Tam, 27 March 2003, Hong Kong.

14. Manuel Puig, *Heartbreak Tango*, trans. Suzanne Jill Levine (London: Arena, 1987), p. 205.

15. Manuel Puig, *Betrayed by Rita Hayworth*, trans. Suzanne Jill Levine (London: Arena, 1987), p. 65.

16. *Heartbreak Tango*, p. 183.

17. Ibid., p. 181.

18. Deleuze, *Difference and Repetition*, p. 110.

19. Ibid.

20. Ibid., p. 111.

21. Quote taken from Haruki Murakami, *Norwegian Wood*, trans. Jay Rubin (London: Vintage, 2000), p. 4.

22. Ngai, 'A Dialogue with Wong Kar-wai'.

23. Interview with Tam.

24. Although another editor, Hai Kit-wai, is also credited, Tam is clearly the senior editor and the one with the artistic responsibility of constructing the picture from the editing table.

25. Interview with Tam.

26. Doyle had shot two of Tam's films, *Burning Snow* (1988) and *My Heart Is That Eternal Rose* (1989).

27. Interview with Tam.

28. Ibid.

29. The music is a big band orchestral rendition, in the style of Cugat, of Ernesto Lecuona's 'Canto Karabali', also known as 'Jungle Drums'.

30. Interview with Tam.

4 – Space–Time Tango

1. Jin Yong is the pseudonym of Louis Cha (Zha Liangyong), b. 1923 in China's Zhejiang province. He started his career as a journalist in Shanghai, and went to Hong Kong in 1948. He founded the newspaper *Ming Pao* in Hong Kong, and started writing martial arts novels in 1955. He has written fifteen novels to date. Most of his novels were serialised in his own newspaper and began a trend of so-called 'new school' *wuxia*. His novels (several of which have been translated into English) have since the late 1950s been popular sources for movie adaptations.

2. Wong himself claimed that he shot it in six weeks. See Mary Jane Amato and J. Greenberg, 'Swimming in Winter: An Interview with Wong Kar-wai', *Kabinet*, no. 5 (Summer 2000), <www.kabinet.org/magazine/issue5/wkw1.html>.

3. See 'Jiujing Wang Jiawei you Shenme Nengnai?' ('The Extent of Wong Kar-wai's Skill'), *Dianying Shuangzhou Kan (City Entertainment)*, no. 397 (30 June–13 July 1994), p. 43.

4. A third story was written but never filmed, and this became the basis of Wong's fifth film, *Fallen Angels*.

5. 'The Extent of Wong Kar-wai's Skill', p. 43.

6. This and other translations of Murakami's short stories are easily resourced on the internet. See <www.geocities.com/oskabe_yoshio/Haruki/Stories-E.html>. Other stories by Murakami which may have influenced *Chungking Express* are the short story 'A Slow Boat to China' and the novel

Norwegian Wood (the Japanese and
Chinese titles of *Norwegian Wood* are
rendered as 'Norwegian Forest', thus the
Chinese title 'Chungking Forest' is
seemingly an allusion to Murakami's
novel). Wong himself is somewhat coy in
response to questions about Murakami's
influence on his films. For example, in
an interview published in the Hong Kong
film magazine *City Entertainment* in
September 1994, he said:

> Maybe in the use of numbers and
> time, we are similar ... but if you were
> to say Murakami influenced me, you
> might as well say I was influenced by
> Camus ... The only thing I have in
> common with Murakami is that we are
> both men with emotion.

See 'Wang Jiawei de Ta yu Ta' ('The This
and That of Wong Kar-wai'), *Dianying
Shuangzhou Kan (City Entertainment)*,
no. 402 (8–21 September 1994), p. 44.

7. See 'The Extent of Wong Kar-wai's
Skill', p. 43.

8. Noël Burch, *Theory of Film Practice*,
trans. Helen R. Lane (London: Secker
and Warburg, 1973), p. 15.

9. Ibid.

10. Bergson's concept of *durée* understood
in relation to the cinema as interpreted
through the theories of Gilles Deleuze is
covered in Ronald Bogue's exegesis on
Deleuze: see 'Chapter One: Bergson and
Cinema', in Bogue, *Deleuze on Cinema*
(New York and London: Routledge,
2003), pp. 11–39.

11. 'The Extent of Wong Kar-wai's Skill',
p. 42.

12. See Gilles Deleuze, *Difference and
Repetition*, trans. Paul Patton (London

and New York: Continuum, 1994),
p. 2.

13. Wong did reveal, however, that he edited
the first 'Chungking' episode, while
Chang edited the second 'Express'
episode. See 'The This and That of Wong
Kar-wai', p. 42.

14. Herbert Read, *A Concise History of
Modern Painting* (London: Thames &
Hudson, 1974), p. 109.

15. See Gilles Deleuze, *Cinema 1: The
Movement Image*, trans. Hugh Tomlinson
and Barbara Habberjam (Minneapolis,
MN: University of Minnesota Press,
2001), p. 4.

16. Read, A. *Concise History of Modern
Painting*, p. 110.

5 – Wong's Biographical Histories of Knights Errant

1. 'Wang Jiawei de Ta yu Ta' ('The This and
That of Wong Kar-wai'), *Dianying
Shuangzhou Kan (City Entertainment)*,
no. 402 (8–21 September 1994), p. 42.
An abridged version of this interview is
translated and reprinted in Wimal
Dissanayake, *Wong Kar-wai's Ashes of
Time* (Hong Kong: Hong Kong University
Press, 2003), pp. 149–58. However, all
passages quoted here are my own
translations.

2. When Wong resumed working on *Ashes
of Time*, he apparently shot all the scenes
with Maggie Cheung in Hong Kong, on
interior sets built in Yuen Long.

3. 'The This and That of Wong Kar-wai',
p. 42.

4. For an account of the production history
of the film, see Dissanayake, *Wong Kar-
wai's Ashes of Time*, pp. 18–21.

5. 'The This and That of Wong Kar-wai',
    p. 46.
6. Interview with Patrick Tam, 27 March
    2003, Hong Kong.
7. Burton Watson, *Records of the Grand
    Historian of China* (New York and
    London: Columbia University Press,
    1961), in two volumes.
8. Sima Qian quotation translated by James
    Liu in Liu, *The Chinese Knight Errant*
    (Chicago, IL: University of Chicago
    Press, 1967), pp. 14–15.
9. Interview with Tam.
10. 'The This and That of Wong Kar-wai',
    p. 40.
11. Ibid.
12. Chen Mo, *Daoguang Jianying Mengtaiqi –
    Zhongguo Wuxia Dianying Lun (Montage of
    Swordplay and Swordfighters: A Treatise on
    Chinese Martial Arts Cinema)* (Beijing:
    China Film Press, 1996), p. 500.
13. 'The This and That of Wong Kar-wai',
    p. 40.
14. Ibid.
15. Ackbar Abbas, *Hong Kong: Culture and
    the Politics of Disappearance* (Hong Kong:
    Hong Kong University Press, 1997),
    p. 58.
16. Michel Foucault, 'Nietzsche, Genealogy,
    History', in Donald F. Bouchard (ed.),
    *Language, Counter-Memory, Practice:
    Selected Essays and Interviews by Michel
    Foucault* (Ithaca, NY: Cornell University
    Press, 1977), p. 154.
17. See, for example, Lisa Odham Stokes
    and Michael Hoover's analysis of *The
    Bride with White Hair* and *Ashes of Time* in
    City on Fire: Hong Kong Cinema (London
    and New York: Verso, 1999), pp. 108–14
    and pp. 187–93.

18. Stephen Ching-kiu Chan, 'Figures of
    Hope and the Filmic Imaginary of
    Jianghu in Contemporary Hong Kong
    Cinema', in John Nguyet Erni (ed.),
    *Cultural Studies: Theorizing Politics,
    Politicizing Theory, Special Issue: Becoming
    (Postcolonial) Hong Kong*, vol. 15,
    nos 3–4 (July–October 2001), p. 500.
19. Ibid.
20. 'The This and That of Wong Kar-wai',
    p. 42.
21. The quote is a paraphrasing of a well-
    known anecdote from the autobiography
    of Hui Neng, the sixth patriarch of Zen
    Buddhism, contained in the *Platform
    Sutra*. Hui Neng had come across two
    monks arguing over a fluttering
    pennant. Was it the wind or the pennant
    that was in motion? Neither, said Hui
    Neng. What actually moved was their
    own mind. For a comment on Wong's
    alteration of the original quotation, see
    Dissanayake, *Wong Kar-wai's Ashes of
    Time*, p. 38.
22. Charles Baudelaire, *Les Fleurs du mal*
    (London: Picador, 1987), p. 128.
23. 'The This and That of Wong Kar-wai',
    p. 42.

6 – Pathos Angelical

1. 'Wang Jiawei de Yizhang Yingbi' ('Wong
    Kar-wai and a Coin'), *Dianying
    Shuangzhou Kan (City Entertainment)*,
    no. 427 (24 August–6 September 1995) ,
    p. 35.
2. See Gilles Deleuze, *Difference and
    Repetition*, trans. Paul Patton (London
    and New York: Continuum, 1994), p. 41.
3. 'Wong Kar-wai and a Coin', p. 33.
4. Ibid.

5. Julia Kristeva, 'Word, Dialogue and Novel', in Toril Moi (ed.), *The Kristeva Reader* (New York: Columbia University Press, 1986), p. 45.

6. Wang Jiawei de Ta yu Ta' ('The This and That of Wong Kar-wai'), *Dianying Shuangzhou Kan (City Entertainment)*, no. 402 (8–21 September 1994), p. 42.

7. Kristeva, 'Word, Dialogue and Novel', p. 53.

8. Wong tends to play in-jokes on his camera crew when conferring names on his fictional characters. Wong Chi-ming is the name of the gaffer in *Fallen Angels*. In *Happy Together*, the names of Lai Yiu-fai (Tony Leung) and Ho Po-wing (Leslie Cheung) are those of a gaffer and a focus-puller who worked on the film.

9. Kristeva, 'Word, Dialogue and Novel', p. 48.

10. Italo Calvino, *Invisible Cities* (London: Picador, 1979), p. 14.

11. Ibid.

12. See 'Wong Kar-wai and a Coin', p. 34.

13. Ackbar Abbas, *Hong Kong: Culture and the Politics of Disappearance* (Hong Kong: Hong Kong University Press, 1997), p. 49.

14. Kristeva, 'Word, Dialogue and Novel', p. 39.

15. Ibid., p. 37.

7 – Wong's Buenos Aires Affair

1. Pang Yi-ping, 'Chunguang Zhaxie: 97 Qian Rang Women Kuaile Zai Yiqi' ('Happy Together: Let's Be Happy Together before '97'), *Dianying Shuangzhou Kan (City Entertainment)*, no. 473 (29 May–11 June 1997), p. 41.

2. See Christopher Doyle, *Don't Try for Me Argentina: Photographic Journal* (Hong Kong: City Entertainment, 1997).

3. 'Let's Be Happy Together before '97', p. 41.

4. Ibid.

5. Lau Tsak-yuen, 'Happy Together with Leslie', *Dianying Shuangzhou Kan (City Entertainment)*, no. 474 (12–25 June 1997), p. 33.

6. 'Let's Be Happy Together before '97', p. 42.

7. From *Buenos Aires Zero Degree* (1999), directed by Kwan Pun-leung and Amos Lee, an hour-long documentary on the making of *Happy Together*.

8. 'Let's Be Happy Together before '97', p. 41.

9. As shown in the documentary *Buenos Aires Zero Degree*, Wong toyed with several storylines after dropping the idea of filming a version of Puig's novel, although these stories appear to have evolved from the original intention of adapting the novel. The first storyline concerned Tony Leung's arrival in Buenos Aires, where, having been told by the cops that his father is in trouble, he goes in search of his father's ex-lover, who turns out to be a man.

10. Wong has stated that all his films revolve around this one theme. See 'Let's Be Happy Together before '97', p. 44.

11. Ibid., p. 42.

12. Ibid., p. 44.

13. Julio Cortázar, *Hopscotch*, trans. Gregory Rabassa (New York: Pantheon Books, 1966), p. 17.

14. Ibid., p. 13.

15. Ibid., p. 36.

16. Ibid., p. 13.

17. Ibid.

18. There is a brief flashback from Leslie
Cheung's perspective, which is shown
in colour and occurs later in the film.
As Wong describes it, the black-and-
white and colour sequences denote the
psychological feelings of the characters
as well as the reversed seasons: black
and white to suggest the cold of the
summer season (actually winter in the
southern hemisphere), and colour to
suggest the warmth of winter
(summer). See 'Let's Be Happy
Together before '97', p. 42. Following
this line of reasoning, Cheung's colour
flashback represents a 'warm' memory
in his mind, while Leung's black-and-
white flashbacks are for him a 'cold'
memory.

19. Edward Lam, 'Chunguang Beihou,
Kuaile Jintou' ('Behind Spring
Brilliance, the End of Happiness'),
*Dianying Shuangzhou Kan (City
Entertainment)*, no. 495 (2–15 April
1998), p. 81.

20. Ibid.

21. See also Doyle's *Don't Try for Me
Argentina*, which includes two pictures of
Cheung preened and powdered in
female make-up wearing mother-of-
pearl sunglasses, along with Doyle's
comment that 'Leslie looks great as a
Redhead ... in high heels, he walks like a
trick-tired whore.'

22. Dialogue quoted from Manuel Puig, *Kiss
of the Spider Woman*, trans. Thomas
Colchie (London: Arena, 1984),
pp. 243–4.

23. Ibid., p. 261.

24. See Fredric Jameson, 'Postmodernism,
or The Cultural Logic of Late
Capitalism', *New Left Review*, no. 146
(1984), p. 53.

25. 'Let's Be Happy Together before '97',
p. 44.

8 – Betrayed by Maggie Cheung

1. See Pang Yi-ping, 'Chunguang Zhaxie:
97 Qian Rang Women Kuaile Zai Yiqi'
('Happy Together: Let's Be Happy
Together before '97'), *Dianying
Shuangzhou Kan (City Entertainment)*,
no. 473 (29 May–11 June 1997), p. 44.

2. Ibid.

3. See the interview with Wong Kar-wai in
the 'Extras' of the French DVD edition
of *In the Mood for Love*, distributed by
TF1 Video/Ocean Films.

4. The English title was not conferred until
much later, when Wong had chanced
upon Bryan Ferry's new version of the
1930s standard 'I'm in the Mood for
Love' (composed by Dorothy Fields and
Jimmy McHugh). The song, however, is
not used in the film, though it features
in the promotional trailers and teasers.
The Chinese title, 'Huayang Nianhua'
(which Wong translates as 'The Age of
Flowers') was already in use as early as
1998; see *Dianying Shuangzhou Kan (City
Entertainment)*, no. 495 (2–15 April
1998), p. 18.

5. Interview with Wong, French DVD.

6. Ibid.

7. Interview with Tony Leung, *Dianying
Shuangzhou Kan (City Entertainment)*,
no. 559 (14–27 September 2000),
p. 31.

8. Interview with Wong, French DVD.

9. Interview with Tony Leung, *Dianying Shuangzhou Kan.*

10. Marcel Proust, *Remembrance of Things Past, Vol. One*, trans. C. K. Scott Moncrieff and Terence Kilmartin (London: Penguin Books, 1989), pp. 179–80.

11. Ibid., p. 179.

12. See Tony Rayns, 'In the Mood for Edinburgh', *Sight and Sound* (August 2000), p. 17.

13. See Liu Yichang, *Jiutu [The Drunkard]* (Hong Kong: Jinshi, 2000), p. 1. The novel is about a Shanghainese writer in Hong Kong lamenting his plight of making a living through writing martial arts novels for serialisation in newspapers, and is typically full of descriptions of Shanghai (and Singapore) nostalgia.

14. Interview with Wong, French DVD.

15. Ibid.

16. Manuel Puig, *Heartbreak Tango*, trans. Suzanne Jill Levine (London: Arena, 1987), p. 125.

17. Julio Cortázar, *Cronopios and Famas*, trans. Paul Blackburn (New York: New Direction Books, 1999), p. 21.

9 – Wong's Time Odyssey

1 See Winnie Chung, 'Dialogue with Wong Kar-wai', *Hollywood Reporter*, 19 May, 2004.

2 See *Beijing Chenbao (Beijing Morning Post)*, <www.morningpost.com.cn/culture/040927whl.htm>, 27 September 2004. See also Jimmy Ngai, 'Wang Jiawei Liushi Niandai Sanbu Qu' ('Wong Kar-wai's The Sixties Trilogy'), *Jet*, vol. 26 (October 2004), pp. 51–2.

3 *Beijing Chenbao (Beijing Morning Post)*, ibid.

4 See Tsang Fan, 'Journey to 2046/2047', *Hao Wai (City Magazine)*, issue 337 (October 2004), p. 191.

5 A Hong Kong Chinese daily reports that the Japanese version may be slightly longer, containing more scenes of Kimura making love to Faye Wong. See *Mingpao*, 5 October 2004. The version shown in Cannes ran for 123 minutes and seemed unfinished according to Derek Elley, writing in his *Variety* review. See Elley, '2046', *Variety* (31 May–6 June, 2004), p. 23. This suggests that there will undoubtedly be many deleted scenes that could find their way into the special features section of a future DVD edition of the film. From press reports, it is known that Wong shot many scenes that were not used, including a whole section describing Chow Mo-wan's marriage to a Chinese woman played by Zhang Jiamin (Carmen Zhang). The sci-fi scenes featuring Thai actor Bird Thongchai MacIntyre and Takuya Kimura also seem severely truncated in the finished film, suggesting that Wong had probably shot more than he was finally inclined or was able to use.

6 See Di Shiwen, review of *2046*, *Xingdao Ribao (Singtao Daily)*, 2 October 2004.

7 See Jimmy Ngai '2046, 5 Years: Making Of', *Hao Wai (City Magazine)*, issue 337 (October 2004), pp. 196–7.

8 Osamu Dazai, *No Longer Human*, trans. Donald Keene (New York: New Directions, 1958), p. 68.

10 – Mini-Projects and Conclusion

1   See 'Tinseltown Tie-up', *South China Morning Post* (8 October 2003).

2   Other press reports indicate that Wong is also contemplating a film version of *The Protein Girl* after the novel by Taiwanese author Wang Wenhua, to feature South Korean actress Song Hye-kyo.

3   The monologue, along with other lines from the film, is quoted verbatim from the soundtrack. The screenplay of *The Follow* was written by Andrew Kevin Walker.

4   The Raymond Chandler reference is alluded to by Wong himself in his commentary accompanying *The Follow*, available online at <www.bmwfilms.com>.

5   On the Lacoste website <www.lacoste.com>.

6   Downloadable on the DJ Shadow website <www.djshadow.com>.

7   Wong has also shot commercials for the Japanese fashion designer Takeo Kikuchi, a Korean cosmetics company SK-II and reportedly, his latest for a French cellphone company. I have been unable to see these commercials and have therefore left them out of this discussion.

8   See the interview with Wong, 'Dakai Goutong Wang Jiawei' ('Opening Communication Wong Kar-wai'), in *Dianying Shuangzhou Kan (City Entertainment)*, no. 485 (13–26 November, 1997), p. 15.

9   Arif Dirlik, 'The Global in the Local', in Rob Wilson and Wimal Dissanayake (eds), *Global Local: Production and the Transnational Imaginary* (Durham, NC: Duke University, 1996).

10 Ibid., p. 32.

BIBLIOGRAPHY

Abbas, Ackbar. *Hong Kong: Culture and the Politics of Disappearance* (Hong Kong: Hong Kong University Press, 1997).

Amato, Mary Jane and J. Greenberg. 'Swimming in Winter: An Interview with Wong Kar-wai', published in the online magazine *Kabinet*, no. 5 (Summer 2000), <www.kabinet.org/magazine/issue5/wkw1.html>.

Baudelaire, Charles. *Les Fleurs du mal* (London: Picador, 1987).

Bear, Liza. 'Wong Kar-wai', *Bomb Magazine*, no. 75 (Spring 2001).

Bogue, Ronald. *Deleuze on Cinema* (New York and London: Routledge, 2003).

Bordwell, David. *Planet Hong Kong* (Cambridge, MA and London: Harvard University Press, 2000).

Burch, Noël. *Theory of Film Practice*, trans. Helen R. Lane (London: Secker and Warburg, 1973).

Calvino, Italo. *Invisible Cities* (London: Picador, 1979).

Chan Ching-kiu, Stephen. 'Figures of Hope and the Filmic Imaginary of Jianghu in Contemporary Hong Kong Cinema', *Cultural Studies: Theorizing Politics, Politicizing Theory, Special Issue: Becoming (Postcolonial)* Hong Kong, ed. John Nguyet Erni, vol. 15, nos. 3–4 (July–October 2001).

Chung, Winnie. 'Dialogue with Wong Kar-wai', *Hollywood Reporter*, 19 May 2004.

Cortázar, Julio. *Hopscotch*, trans. Gregory Rabassa (New York: Pantheon Books, 1966).

Cortázar, Julio. *Cronopios and Famas*, trans. Paul Blackburn (New York: New Direction Books, 1999).

Dazai, Osamu. *The Setting Sun*, trans. Donald Keene (New York: New Directions, 1956)

Dazai, Osamu. *No Longer Human*, trans. Donald Keene (New York: New Directions, 1958).

Deleuze, Gilles. *Difference and Repetition*, trans. Paul Patton (London and New York: Continuum, 1994).

Deleuze, Gilles. *Cinema 1: The Movement Image*, trans. Hugh Tomlinson and Barbara Habberjam (Minneapolis, MN: University of Minnesota Press, 2001).

Dirlik, Arif. 'The Global in the Local', in Rob Wilson and Wimal Dissanayake (eds), *Global Local: Production and the Transnational*

Imaginary (Durham, NC: Duke University. 1996).

Dissanayake, Wimal. *Wong Kar-wai's Ashes of Time* (Hong Kong: Hong Kong University Press, 2003).

Doyle, Christopher. *Don't Try for Me Argentina: A Photographic Journal* (Hong Kong: City Entertainment, 1997).

Eliot, T. S. *The Waste Land and Other Poems* (London: Faber, 1972).

Elley, Derek. '2046', *Variety* (31 May–6 June 2004).

Foucault, Michel. *Language, Counter-Memory, Practice: Selected Essays and Interviews by Michel Foucault*, ed. Donald F. Bouchard (Ithaca, NY: Cornell University Press, 1977).

Jameson, Fredric. 'Postmodernism, or The Cultural Logic of Late Capitalism', *New Left Review*, no. 146 (1984).

Kristeva, Julia. 'Word, Dialogue and Novel', *The Kristeva Reader*, ed. by Toril Moi (New York: Columbia University Press, 1986).

Lalanne, Jean-Marc, Martinez, David, Abbas, Ackbar and Jimmy Ngai. *Wong Kar-wai* (Paris: Dis Voir, 1997).

Murakami, Haruki. *Norwegian Wood*, trans. Jay Rubin (London: Vintage, 2000).

Murakami, Haruki. *Hard-Boiled Wonderland and the End of the World* (London: Vintage, 2001).

Proust, Marcel. *Remembrance of Things Past, Vol. One*, trans. C. K. Scott Moncrieff and Terence Kilmartin (London: Penguin Books, 1989).

Puig, Manuel. *The Buenos Aires Affair*, trans. Suzanne Jill Levine (New York: E. P. Dutton, 1976).

Puig, Manuel. *Kiss of the Spider Woman*, trans. Thomas Colchie (London: Arena, 1984).

Puig, Manuel. *Betrayed by Rita Hayworth*, trans. Suzanne Jill Levine (London: Arena, 1987).

Puig, Manuel. *Heartbreak Tango*, trans. Suzanne Jill Levine (London: Arena, 1987).

Rayns, Tony. 'In the Mood for Edinburgh', *Sight and Sound* (August 2000).

Read, Herbert. *A Concise History of Modern Painting* (London: Thames & Hudson, 1974).

Stokes, Lisa Odham and Michael Hoover. *City on Fire: Hong Kong Cinema* (London and New York: Verso, 1999).

Tambling, Jeremy. *Wong Kar-wai's Happy Together* (Hong Kong: Hong Kong University Press, 2003).

Teo, Stephen. *Hong Kong Cinema: The Extra Dimensions* (London: BFI, 1997).

Tirard, Laurent. *Moviemakers' Master Class: Private Lessons from the World's Foremost Directors* (New York: Faber and Faber, 2002).

In Chinese

Chen Mo. *Daoguang Jianying Mengtaiqi – Zhongguo Wuxia Dianying Lun (Montage of Swordplay and Swordfighters: A Treatise on Chinese Martial Arts Cinema)* (Beijing: China Film Press, 1996).

Cheung Chi-sing. '"A Fei Zhengzhuan": Wogan Wosi' ('My Feelings and Thoughts on "Days of Being Wild"'), *Dianying Shuangzhou Kan (City Entertainment)*, no. 308 (17–30 January 1991).

'Dakai Goutong Wang Jiawei' ('Opening Communication with Wong Kar-wai') *Dianying Shuangzhou Kan (City Entertainment)*, no. 485 (13–26 November 1997).

'Dudang Yimian de Wang Jiawei' ('Wong Kar-wai Takes Charge'), *Dianying Shuangzhou Kan (Film Biweekly)*, no. 244 (28 July 1988).

Interview with Tony Leung, *Dianying Shuangzhou Kan (City Entertainment)*, no. 559 (14–27 September 2000).

Jin Yong. *Shediao Yingxiong Zhuan [The Eagle Shooting Heroes, aka The Legend of the Condor Heroes]* in four volumes (Beijing: Sanlian Shudian, 1999).

'Jiujing Wang Jiawei you Shenme Nengnai?' ('The Extent of Wong Kar-wai's Skill'), *Dianying Shuangzhou Kan (City Entertainment)*, no. 397 (30 June–13 July 1994).

Lam, Edward (Lam Yik-wah). 'Chunguang Beihou, Kuaile Jintou' ('Behind Spring Brilliance, the End of Happiness'), *Dianying Shuangzhou Kan (City Entertainment)*, no. 495 (2–15 April 1998).

Lau Tsak-yuen. 'Happy Together with Leslie', *Dianying Shuangzhou Kan (City Entertainment)*, no. 474 (12–25 June 1997).

Lee, Bono (Lee Chiu-hing). *Xianggang Hou Modeng [Hong Kong Post-modern]* (Hong Kong: Zhinanzhen, 2002).

Lee, Bono and Lawrence Pun,(eds). *Wang Jiawei de Yinghua Shijie [The Cinematic World of Wong Kar-wai]* (Hong Kong: Joint Publishing, 2004).

Liu Yichang. *Duidao [Intersections, aka Tête-Bêche]* (Hong Kong: Holdery Publishing, 2000).

Liu Yichang. *Jiutu [The Drunkard]* (Hong Kong: Jinshi, 2000).

Ngai, Jimmy (Ngai Siu-yan). 'All About "A Fei Zhengzhuan", Yu Wang Jiawei Duihua' ('All About "Days of Being Wild": A Dialogue with Wong Kar-wai'), *Dianying Shuangzhou Kan (City Entertainment)*, no. 305 (6–19 December 1990).

Ngai, Jimmy. 'Romance of the Individual: A Fei Zhengzhuan', *Dianying Shuangzhou Kan (City Entertainment)*, no. 310 (14–27 February 1991).

Ngai, Jimmy. '2046, 5 Years: Making Of', *Haowai (City Magazine)*, issue 337 (October 2004).

Ngai, Jimmy. 'Wang Jiawei Liushi Niandai Sanbu Qu' (*Wong Kar-wai's The Sixties Trilogy*), *Jet*, vol. 26 (October 2004).

Pang Yi-ping. 'Chunguang Zhaxie: 97 Qian Rang Women Kuaile Zai Yiqi' ('Happy Together: Let's Be Happy Together before '97'), *Dianying Shuangzhou Kan* (*City Entertainment*), no. 473 (29 May–11 June 1997).

Tianshi. 'The Days of Being Wild: Feilübin Waijing Bari' ('The Days of Being Wild: Eight-Day Location Shooting in the Philippines'), *Dianying Shuangzhou Kan* (*City Entertainment*), no. 306 (20 December – 2 January, 1990).

Tsang Fan, 'Journey to 2046/2047', *Hao Wai* (*City Magazine*), issue 337 (October 2004).

'Wang Jiawei de Ta yu Ta' ('The This and That of Wong Kar-wai'), *Dianying Shuangzhou Kan* (*City Entertainment*), no. 402 (8–21 September 1994).

'Wang Jiawei de Yizhang Yingbi' ('Wong Kar-wai and a Coin'), *Dianying Shuangzhou Kan* (*City Entertainment*), no. 427 (24 August–6 September 1995).

'Wang Jiawei Zongtan "Wangjiao Kamen"' ('Wong Kar-wai on "As Tears Go By"'), *Dianying Shuangzhou Kan* (*Film Biweekly*), no. 241 (16 June 1988).

FILMOGRAPHY

Feature Films

As Tears Go By
(*Wangjiao Kamen*, 1988)

Director/Screenplay: Wong Kar-wai
Producer: Rover Tang
Executive Producer: Alan Tang
Director of Photography: Andrew Lau
Production Designer: William Chang
Editors: Peter Chiang, Patrick Tam
    (uncredited), William Chang
    (uncredited)
Music: Danny Chung
Cast: Andy Lau, Maggie Cheung, Jacky
    Cheung, Alex Man, Wong Ang, Wong
    Bun, Chan Chi-fai, William Chang,
    Kong To-hoi
Production Company: In-Gear
Running Time: 100 minutes
Colour

Days of Being Wild
(*A Fei Zhengzhuan*, 1990)

Director/Screenplay: Wong Kar-wai
Producer: Rover Tang
Executive Producer: Alan Tang
Director of Photography: Christopher
    Doyle
Production Designer: William Chang
Editors: Patrick Tam, Hai Kit-wai

Sound Recordist: Chan Wai-hung
Cast: Leslie Cheung, Maggie Cheung,
    Andy Lau, Carina Lau, Jacky Cheung,
    Rebecca Pan, Tony Leung Chiu-wai
Production Company: In-Gear
Running Time: 92 minutes
Colour

Chungking Express
(*Chongqing Senlin*, 1994)

Director/Screenplay: Wong Kar-wai
Producer: Chan Ye-cheng
Director of Photography: Christopher
    Doyle
Production Designer: William Chang
Editor: William Chang
Music: Frankie Chan
Cast: Takeshi Kaneshiro, Brigitte Lin,
    Tony Leung Chiu-wai, Faye Wong,
    Valerie Chow
Production Company: Jet Tone
Running Time: 90 minutes (Hong
    Kong version), 102 minutes
    (international version)
Colour

Ashes of Time
(*Dongxie Xidu*, 1994)

Director/Screenplay: Wong Kar-wai
Producer: Tsai Mui-ho

Executive Producer: Chan Pui-wah
Director of Photography: Christopher
    Doyle
Production Designer: William Chang
Editors: Patrick Tam, William Chang,
    Hai Kit-wai, Kwong Chi-leung
Music: Frankie Chan, Roel A. Garcia
Martial Arts Director: Sammo Hung
Cast: Leslie Cheung, Tony Leung Ka-
    fai, Brigitte Lin, Tony Leung Chiu-
    wai, Jacky Cheung, Carina Lau,
    Maggie Cheung, Charlie Young, Bai
    Li, Ni Xing, Siu Tak-fu
Production Company: Jet Tone, Scholar
    Films, in association with Beijing
    Film Studio, Tsui Siu-ming
    Productions and Pony Canyon
Running Time: 95 minutes
Colour

Fallen Angels
(*Duoluo Tianshi*, 1995)

Director/Screenplay: Wong Kar-wai
Producer: Jeff Lau
Executive Producer: Jacky Pang
    Yee-wah
Director of Photography: Christopher
    Doyle
Production Designer: William Chang
Editors: William Chang, Wong
    Ming-lam
Music: Frankie Chan, Roel A. Garcia
Cast: Leon Lai, Michele Reis, Takeshi
    Kaneshiro, Charlie Young, Karen

Mok, Chan Fai-hung, Chan Man-lei
Production Company: Jet Tone
Running Time: 101 minutes
Colour

Happy Together
(*Chunguang Zhaxie*, 1997)

Producer/Director/Screenplay: Wong
    Kar-wai
Executive Producer: Chan Ye-cheng
Director of Photography: Christopher
    Doyle
Production Designer: William Chang
Editors: William Chang, Wong Ming-lam
Music: Danny Chung
Cast: Leslie Cheung, Tony Leung Chiu-
    wai, Chang Chen
Production Company: Block 2 Pictures,
    Prenom H. Co., Seowoo Film Co.,
    Jet Tone
Running Time: 97 minutes
Colour

In the Mood for Love
(*Huayang Nianhua*, 2000)

Director/Screenplay: Wong Kar-wai
Executive Producer: Chan Ye-cheng
Directors of Photography: Christopher
    Doyle, Mark Lee Ping-bin
Production Designer: William Chang
Editor: William Chang
Original Music: Michael Galasso
Music: Shigeru Umebayashi
Cast: Tony Leung Chiu-wai, Maggie
    Cheung, Rebecca Pan, Lei Zhen, Siu

Ping-lam, Chan Man-lei, Chin
Tsi-ang
Production Company: Block 2 Pictures,
Paradis Films, Jet Tone
Running Time: 95 minutes
Colour

2046 (2004)

Director/Screenplay: Wong Kar-wai
Producers: Wong Kar-wai, Yimou
Zhang
Director of Photography: Christopher
Doyle
Production Designer/Editor: William
Chang
Music: Peer Raben, Shigeru Umebayashi
Cast: Tony Leung Chiu-wai, Li Gong,
Takuya Kimura, Faye Wong, Ziyi
Zhang, Carina Lau, Chen Chang
Production Company: Block 2 Pictures,
Paradis Films, Orly Films, Jet Tone
Running Time: 120 minutes
Colour

Other

The Motorola commercial (1998)

Director: Wong Kar-wai
Director of Photography: Christopher
Doyle
Production Designer: William Chang
Cast: Faye Wong, Tadanobu Asano
Running Time: 3 minutes

The Follow (2001)

Director: Wong Kar-wai
Screenplay: Andrew Kevin Walker
Director of Photography: Harris
Savides
Production Designer/Editor: William
Chang
Music: 'Unicornio'
Cast: Clive Owen, Adriana Lima,
Mickey Rourke, Forest Whitaker
Production commissioned by BMW
Running Time: 8.47 minutes

The Lacoste commercial (2002)

Director: Wong Kar-wai
Director of Photography: Eric Gautier
Music: Shigeru Umebayashi
Cast: Chang Chen, Diane MacMahon
Production Company: Jet Tone (Hong
Kong), Entropie (France)
Running Time: (in three formats) 30
seconds, 40 seconds, 1 minute

'Six Days' (DJ Shadow music video, 2002)

Director: Wong Kar-wai
Director of Photography: Christopher
Doyle
Music: DJ Shadow
Cast: Chang Chen, Danielle Graham
Running Time: 3.41 minutes

INDEX

List of Illustrations

Whilst considerable effort has been made to correctly identify the copyright holders this has not been possible in all cases. We apologise for any apparent negligence and any omissions or corrections brought to our attention will be remedied in any future editions.

As Tears Go By, In-Gear Film Production Co. Ltd; *Days of Being Wild*, In-Gear Film Production Co. Ltd; *Chungking Express*, Jet Tone; *Ashes of Time*, Scholar Films/Jet Tone/Tsui Siu-ming Production/Beijing Film Studio/Pony Canyon; *Fallen Angels*, Jet Tone; *Happy Together*, Jet Tone/Block 2 Pictures/ Prenom H. Co./Seawoo Film Co.; *In the Mood for Love*, © Block 2 Pictures; *2046*, Block 2 Pictures/Paradis Films/Orly Films/Jet Tone.